PRENTICE HAL

Constitution Study Guide

CONSULTANT

Dr. Christine Compston

Author of
Earl Warren: Justice for All

Prentice
Hall

Needham, Massachussetts
Upper Saddle River, New Jersey
Glenview, Illinois

Cover Design: Roberto Portocarrero

Photo Credits
Corbis, cover; Steve Chenn/Corbis, 6; Bettmann/Corbis, 9, 13, 16, 22, 30, 32, 46, 56, 67, 78; The Granger Collection, New York, 18; Virginia Museum of Fine Arts, Richmond/Gift of Edgar William and Bernice Chrysler Garbisch/Ron Jennings photo, 29; Photri, Inc., 38; VEC Archives, 49; AFP/Corbis, 60; J. McGuire/Washington Stock Photo, Inc., 71; Courtesy U.S. Supreme Court, 74.

CONSTITUTION STUDY GUIDE

Needham, Massachussetts
Upper Saddle River, New Jersey
Glenview, Illinois

© 2001 by Prentice Hall, Inc., Upper Saddle River, New Jersey 07548

12 13 14 15 16 17 18   09 08 07 06

ISBN 0-13-043835-9

Table of Contents

Introduction

You and the Constitution

To appreciate the enormous impact the U.S. Constitution has on your life, imagine for a moment that it does not exist. What difference would this make?

The United States might have remained the loose confederation of independent states, each one making its own decisions about political, social, and economic matters. Some states, for example, might give women the right to vote, serve on juries, and to receive equal pay for their work; others might not. Some states might allow the government to establish and pay for religious education; others might not.

In terms of the day-to-day lives of individuals, the U.S. Constitution—both the original document and amendments that have been added in the past 200 years—has a tremendous impact. For example, let's assume you have written a book or produced a CD, and you want to make a profit on your work. The only way that you can be assured that you will earn the money is by obtaining a copyright, which establishes you as the owner of the work. The Constitution protects your right by creating a copyright office where you register your work.

Most countries now have written constitutions—some of them modeled on the U.S. Constitution. What makes the United States different from some of these nations is how and when constitutional provisions are enforced. The U.S. Congress follows the Constitution when it writes laws, the President follows it when administering laws, and the courts when they interpret and apply laws. Individual citizens study the Constitution to learn their responsibilities as well as their rights.

Written more than 200 years ago, and changed only a few times, it is still the legal document that defines our system of government. The Constitution's long history of success is credited to its writers—men who, with a vision of their new nation, created a flexible document that could be adapted as society changed.

How much do you know about the Constitution and the impact it has on your life? The following questions enable you to find out.

How much do you know about the Constitution?

The following questions test your knowledge of how the U.S. Constitution affects the lives of young people. The answer to each question is either "true" or "false," for a total of 10 points.

1. All Americans have an unlimited right to freedom of expression.
2. The U.S. Constitution recognizes that the good of society must outweigh the rights of the individual.
3. A young person can be asked to testify against himself or herself in a juvenile court proceeding.
4. A juvenile has a right to a lawyer if accused of a crime.
5. Minors have the same right to trial by jury as adults.
6. High school students have the right to conduct a political demonstration at school.
7. A principal or superintendent can stop the publication of a school newspaper if it is saying bad things about the school.
8. If a juvenile is arrested, his or her parents must be informed immediately.
9. If a school official searches a student's locker without a search warrant, nothing that is found can be used against the student.
10. Young people have the same rights under the U.S. Constitution as adults.

When you finish the unit on the Constitution, take this quiz again. Your teacher will give you the correct answers to the quiz questions at that time. Give yourself one point for each correct answer. Then compare your two performances on the quiz and rate yourself on the scale below.

9 or 10 right—Constitutional scholar

7 or 8 right—Knowledgeable citizen

5 or 6 right—Average person on the street

4 or fewer right—You are not looking out for your rights!

Constitutional Issues Confront the Lives of Students

Young Americans face constitutional issues that their parents and grandparents never confronted. Views about the rights of minors have changed, and today's young people enjoy many of the constitutional rights and protections of adults. Each of the first four chapters in this guide contains a description of a Supreme Court case involving students. These cases deal with the constitutional rights of young people. Each case presents the arguments for and against the students involved, then asks you to decide how you think the Supreme Court should have ruled in each case.

The U.S. Constitution is a remarkable document. It has served our country well for more than two centuries, and it has also been the model that other governments and organizations have followed. State constitutions commonly parallel the federal document. In the following pages, you will learn how the U.S. Constitution came into being and why it has remained the flexible and enduring law of the land.

PRIMARY SOURCES

"The schoolroom is the first opportunity most citizens have to experience the power of government. The values they learn there, they take with them in life."

—Dissenting opinion,
New Jersey v. T.L.O.

PRIMARY SOURCES

"The fundamental [requirement] of due process is the opportunity to be heard."

—Opinion of the Court,
Goss v. Lopez

The Roots of Constitutional Government

Independence Hall in Philadelphia, Pennsylvania.

About This Chapter

From May 25 to September 17, 1787, the Framers of the Constitution of the United States of America debated, wrote, and revised their nation's future. They labored during the hottest summer months in a building with closed windows and without air conditioning. Outside, hay and gravel were strewn on the cobblestones so that the clatter of passing carriages would not disturb their important discussions.

The ideas that shaped the thinking of the men who wrote the Constitution developed over many years. Abuses that the colonists had endured by the British government influenced the Framers' thinking. So, too, did the philosophies of government that developed in Europe in the 1700s. Other factors that influenced the men who drafted the Constitution were the successes and failures of their early experience with self-government before, during, and after the Revolution. These influences are the subject of this chapter.

1 Americans Declare Their Independence

As you read, think about the answers to these questions:

➤ Why did the colonists rebel against Britain?

➤ How did the colonists establish their independence?

➤ What are the basic human rights demanded in the Declaration of Independence?

From the time of first settlement in Jamestown, Virginia, in the early 1600s until 1776, the American colonies were under European control. Governors in the British colonies, whether appointed by a monarch or proprietor, or selected by the people, ruled the settlements and enforced British laws. In truth, however, colonial governors often allowed the colonists much freedom. This policy, known as salutary neglect, was in place for many decades.

salutary neglect *British policy that allowed American colonists to rule themselves so long as Britain also benefited*

For most of the colonial period, locally elected assemblies decided how to deal with the day-to-day issues that affected the colonists. Members of the assemblies enacted their own laws, including those relating to taxation. Britain, engaged in wars in Europe, permitted this self-rule as long as the colonies supplied Britain with materials for British industries and bought British-made goods. This system satisfied the needs of both Britain and the American colonies for some time. In the mid-1700s, however, relations between the English king and the American colonists grew tense.

The Colonists Rebel

After four long wars against France, Britain was left with a huge war debt. In 1763 King George III and Parliament decided that the colonies should pay taxes to relieve the debt. In addition, Britain began to tax the goods going to or coming from the colonies. The colonists, however, resented the taxes and the interference and disruption of their self-rule. Eventually this conflict developed into the American Revolution. Historians note that three types of problems—economic, social, and political—eventually led to rebellion in 1776.

Parliament *British lawmaking body*

Social Problems.
Among the social problems that existed in the colonies were the following:

- The colonists had become used to solving their own problems.

repeal *to officially withdraw*

representation *elected leadership*

revolutionary *favoring great change*

Continental Congress *group of colonial leaders who debated and implemented action plans regarding the colonists' relations with Britain*

- When local royal authorities attempted to enforce British laws, the colonists became resentful.

Economic Problems. Many of the laws that Parliament made concerned economic ties between Britain and the colonies.

- Britain wanted access to the colonies' raw materials for its own use.
- Britain wanted the colonists to buy only goods made in Britain.
- Britain's insistence that colonists use gold to purchase British goods led to inflation and hardships.

Political Problems. Between 1765 and 1770, Parliament twice placed new taxes on the colonies. Both times the colonists protested and Britain repealed the taxes. But these social and economic tensions had developed into a serious political dispute.

- Because the colonists did not have representation in Parliament, they believed they were being unfairly taxed.
- Colonists believed they were better qualified to govern themselves.
- Support for American independence was growing steadily.

During 1775 and 1776, colonists talked about establishing an independent nation. The writings of several leaders, and resolutions passed by several congresses, expressed and supported this revolutionary mood.

The Call for Independence

In 1776 political thinker and author Thomas Paine wrote a pamphlet titled *Common Sense,* advocating independence. That pamphlet, and the growing support for independence among the colonists, had an effect on the Continental Congress. Elected delegates from the 13 colonies had been meeting since 1775 to decide how to respond to British policies.

Congress Responds. By 1776 more and more members of Congress had come to believe that the colonies must declare independence. In June 1776, the Congress appointed a committee, headed by Thomas Jefferson, to prepare such a declaration. On July 2, Jefferson presented his draft of the Declaration of Independence to the delegates. Two days later, after making some changes to the document, the Second Continental Congress voted to accept it.

Americans State Their Rights and Grievances

The Declaration of Independence contains a statement of basic human rights and government responsibilities, as well as a list of grievances against the British king.

Stating Their Rights. Thomas Jefferson's words expressed the feeling of many colonists. He outlined several basic rights at the beginning of the document.

endow *to grant or provide*

unalienable *incapable of being taken away or transferred to another*

abolish *to put an end to*

Many colonists believed that there were certain basic truths about human beings that all governments must recognize. They are that:

- All men are created equal.
- Government cannot take away certain rights given to people by God or nature.
- Governments are established by human beings to preserve these rights.
- Government receives its power through the consent of the people.
- The people agree to be governed.
- The people have the right to abolish a government that disregards their rights.

Listing Their Grievances. Jefferson also presented a list of injustices in the Declaration of Independence to show how King George had oppressed the colonists. The grievances included:

- Imposing taxes on the colonists without their consent, and
- Cutting off the colonists' trade with all parts of the world.

Declaring War. The Declaration of Independence severed political ties with Britain. In stating their independence from Britain, the colonists were declaring war against that nation. That war, the American Revolution, lasted from 1776 until 1783.

The Declaration stated the principles of a new nation, but it did not provide a plan for the creation of a new government. In 1783 there were few democratic governments in the world. Americans relied on historical examples and their own colonial governments as they hammered out the details of their new government. After years of debate, the delegates met once more—in Philadelphia in 1787—to draft the Constitution of the United States. Remarkably, this plan of government still guides the nation, more than 200 years later.

Thomas Jefferson, admired for his writing skills, was asked to draft the Declaration of Independence. He is shown here conferring with Benjamin Franklin on a draft of the document.

Name _____ **Date** _____

1 Review

1. Defining Constitutional Terms

Write a brief definition for each of the following terms.

a. Continental Congress _____

b. representation _____

c. revolutionary _____

d. repealed _____

e. salutary neglect _____

f. unalienable right _____

2. Reviewing Social Studies Skills: Analyzing a Quotation

Read the quotation below and examine the statements that follow it. Circle the letter next to the statement that best explains the quotation.

"To be always running 3,000 or 4,000 miles with a tale or a petition, waiting four or five months for an answer which, when obtained, requires five or six more [months] to explain it in, will in a few years be looked upon as folly and childishness—there was a time when it was proper, and there is a proper time for it to cease."

—*Thomas Paine in* Common Sense

a. The time when the colonists needed guidance and support from Britain has ended.

b. England is between 3,000 and 4,000 miles from America by land.

c. It takes more than five months to receive mail from Britain.

3. Reviewing the Main Ideas

Using complete sentences, write a brief answer for each of the following questions.

a. Explain why the colonists rebelled against Britain. _____

_____

_____

b. What did the Continental Congress do to establish American independence? _____

_____

_____

c. What are two basic human rights stated in the Declaration of Independence? _____

_____

_____

4. Critical Thinking Skills: Understanding the Constitution

Once the Continental Congress signed the Declaration of Independence, Americans considered the colonies to be free and independent states. Still, the states had to fight against Britain to become a truly independent nation. On a separate sheet of paper, write a paragraph discussing why Britain was against American independence.

European Influences

As you read, think about the answers to these questions:

➤ What important ideas did the ancient Greeks and Romans contribute to the American system of government?

➤ What contributions did the English make to the development of American government?

➤ How did European political philosophers influence the Framers of the U.S. Constitution?

For as long as people have lived in groups, they have needed some type of organization to maintain order. Without order, a society would be in constant chaos. Government creates order in a society. After the Americans declared their independence from Britain in 1776, they needed to form a government. The ideas that shaped the American plan of government came from three main sources.

1. Ancient Greece and Rome
2. English history and British political thinkers
3. European philosophers

From Ancient Greece and Rome

The first societies to experiment with ideas on government that would later influence Americans were ancient Greece and Rome. These ancient societies developed their concepts of democracy and representative government more than 2,000 years ago.

Ancient Greek Democracy. Ancient Greece was organized into city-states, or small independent nations. Athens was one such city-state. For many years, Athens was ruled by a small group of wealthy and powerful men known as the Great Council. Members of the Council passed laws that favored wealthy people like themselves. Between 750 B.C. and 550 B.C., however, this system of rule began to change.

Poorer Athenians, such as farmers and small merchants, believed that the laws made by the Council ignored their interests. Many Greeks wanted to participate in the lawmaking process that affected their lives. Greeks used the term *demos kratia,* which means "government by the people," to describe the concept of democracy.

philosopher *person who seeks wisdom and enlightenment*

PRIMARY SOURCES

"If liberty and equality, as is thought by some, are chiefly to be found in democracy, they will be best attained when all persons alike share in the government to the utmost."

—Aristotle

city-state *independent state consisting of a city and the area surrounding it*

democracy *government by the people*

11

direct democracy *system of government in which people participate directly in decision making through voting on issues*

citizenship *the status of a citizen, or member of a country, with all its duties, rights, and privileges*

eligible *qualified or worthy of being selected*

republic *system of government in which people elect representatives to govern them; also known as representative government*

patrician *member of the Roman upper class who traced his ancestry to a senatorial family in the earliest days of the Roman Republic*

plebeian *member of the general body of Roman citizens, as distinct from the patricians, or upper class*

codify *to arrange according to a system; to set down in writing*

absolute monarch *all-powerful king or queen*

common law *system of law based on accepted customs, traditions, and past decisions*

Gradually, Athenian leaders agreed that more Greeks should be allowed to participate in the Great Council's decision-making process. They developed a political system, now known as a **direct democracy**, in which people not only elected their leaders but also served in the government.

Greek leaders used the concept of **citizenship** to determine who was **eligible** to participate in government. They decided that only men who owned large plots of land were citizens. Women, slaves, and people with little or no property were not considered citizens. Although the Greeks restricted democratic rights to a small portion of the population, the idea of rule by the people was born.

Ancient Roman Republic. Between 750 B.C. and 350 B.C., the Romans established a **republic**, a form of government in which people elect representatives to govern them. At first, only **patricians** were allowed to vote or serve as representatives. Gradually the right to vote was extended to **plebeians**. As more Romans gained the right to vote, they used their new power to bring about other changes in the political system.

Around 450 B.C., Roman citizens demanded that laws governing their lives be written down. They believed that **codified** laws would prevent Roman leaders from abusing their power.

English History Influences American Government

The first European nation to experiment with democracy was Britain. For many centuries, Britain was ruled by an **absolute monarch**. Between 1100 and 1200, however, the English political system began to change.

English Common Law. In the 1100s, King Henry II attempted to expand the power of the monarchy.

- The king established courts throughout the country.
- The king's judges assembled juries to hear cases.
- Royal judges made laws based on the customs of the people.
- Juries used these laws to resolve disputes and to determine a person's guilt or innocence.
- Court decisions were gradually written down and became the basis for **common law**, which applied to all English citizens.

Magna Carta. The expansion of royal power in England did not go unopposed. The king's barons, or noblemen, resented Henry's court system because it took away some of their traditional powers. The power struggle between the king and his barons worsened when King John, who succeeded Henry, placed new taxes on the barons. Finally, in 1215, the barons joined together and forced King John to grant a charter that guaranteed their rights and privileges. This document became known as Magna Carta, or Great Charter, and stated that:

- The king could not place taxes on the barons without the consent of the Great Council, a group of influential barons.
- No free person could be imprisoned without a jury trial.

Despite protecting only a small portion of the British population (the nobility), Magna Carta was a major political achievement. It demonstrated that a monarch's power could be legally limited by the citizens.

Parliament. The creation of the Great Council and the granting of Magna Carta were the first steps in the development of representative government in Britain. The Council, which demanded that the king seek its approval before making decisions, eventually became known as Parliament. The term *parliament* comes from the French word *parler*, which means "to talk." Members of Parliament discussed political issues and policies and presented their views to the king.

By the 1600s, Parliament had become more of an equal partner in the English government, sharing power with the monarchy. Although the king and Parliament shared power, they did not always cooperate with each other.

The Bill of Rights. In the mid-1600s, the power struggle between the king and Parliament led to a civil war. By the 1680s, Parliament had so much power it was able to force King James II from the throne and select his successors, James' daughter Mary and her husband William of Orange. In exchange for the throne, Parliament demanded that William and Mary sign a Bill of Rights, which stated that:

- The monarch could not make or suspend laws without the consent or approval of Parliament.

- The monarch needed the consent of Parliament to raise taxes and maintain an army.

- The monarchy could not interfere in parliamentary elections.

- The monarchy would protect freedom of religion, the right to petition, and other freedoms we see as basic today.

These three events—the granting of Magna Carta, the creation of Parliament, and the enactment of the Bill of Rights—gradually reduced the power of the British monarchy.

King John authorized that handwritten copies of Magna Carta be affixed with his seal and read aloud in public squares.

European Philosophers Influence American Government

During the **Enlightenment** in the 1600s and 1700s, many political philosophers met to discuss their ideas about government. Among the most influential of these were John Locke, Jean Jacques Rousseau, and Baron de Montesquieu.

Locke's Contract Theory. John Locke was an English political thinker and writer. In 1690 he published the *Two Treatises on Government,* in which he explained his contract theory of government. According to Locke:

- Magna Carta and the Bill of Rights protect the natural rights of all British citizens.

- All people have the inalienable "right to life, liberty, and property."

- Government arises from a contract, or agreement, between the ruler and the ruled.

- A ruler has power only as long as he or she has the consent of the governed.

- A ruler can not justly deny people their basic rights to life, liberty, and property.

Rousseau Expands the Contract Theory. In his book titled *The Social Contract,* Jean Jacques Rousseau wrote about an ideal society. Although no such society existed at the time, Rousseau's vision was later adopted by the American colonists. In Rousseau's ideal society:

- People would form a community and make a contract with each other, not with a ruler.

- People would give up some of their freedom in favor of the needs of the majority.

- The community would vote on all decisions, and everyone would live by the community's decisions.

Montesquieu Suggests Limited Government. In his book on government, *The Spirit of Laws,* Baron de Montesquieu developed practical suggestions for creating democratic governments, which he referred to as a system of checks and balances. He also promoted a separation of powers, in which individuals in one branch of government would not hold office in another. He believed that:

- The best way to ensure that the government protects the natural rights of citizens is to limit its powers.

- The best way to limit government's powers is to divide those basic powers among a number of authorities.

Most educated Americans living at the time the Constitution was written were familiar with the political practices of the ancient Greeks and Romans, the British parliamentary system, and the writings of Enlightenment philosophers. The Framers of the U.S. Constitution were deeply affected by the philosophies of government that developed during the previous 2,000 years.

SECTION

2 Review

1. Defining Constitutional Terms
Write a brief definition for each of the following terms.

a. democracy _____

b. direct democracy _____

c. citizenship _____

d. republic _____

e. codify _____

f. absolute monarch _____

g. common law _____

2. Reviewing Social Studies Skills: Understanding Relationships
Draw an arrow from the event in the left column to the effect it produced in the right column.

a. Enlightenment begins	Direct democracy established
b. Poorer Athenians protest	Parliament develops
c. English barons rebel	New ideas about government develop
d. England's Great Council is created	Magna Carta is granted

3. Reviewing the Main Ideas
Using complete sentences, write a brief answer for each of the following questions.

a. In what way did Greek democracy change between 750 B.C. and 550 B.C.? _____

_____

_____

_____

b. What impact did English ideas and practices have on American government? _____

_____

_____

_____

c. How did the ideas of European political philosophers influence the way the Framers wrote the U.S. Constitution?

_____

_____

_____

4. Critical Thinking Skills: Understanding the Constitution
On a separate sheet of paper, write a paragraph to answer the following question.

How is a republic both similar to and different from a direct democracy?

The Need for a New Plan

As you read, think about the answers to these questions:

➤ What problems did the new nation face?

➤ How did the Articles of Confederation limit national government?

➤ What caused American leaders to call for a revision of the Articles of Confederation?

George Washington's military skill and experience were vital as he commanded Americans during the revolution that ended two centuries of British rule over the colonies.

militia *military force that is called up for service during emergencies*

The first attempt by the United States to form a new government, like many new ventures, succeeded in some respects while it failed in others. After a few years, however, the problems facing the new nation had become so serious that American leaders called for a better plan.

Facing Serious Problems

The signing of the Declaration of Independence marked the birth of a new nation. Consisting of the 13 former colonies, the new nation faced three major tasks:

1. Win a war against the British.

2. Organize new state governments.

3. Establish a national government.

Fighting the Revolution. The signing of the Declaration of Independence sparked a full-scale war against Britain, one of the most powerful nations in the world. The struggle was made more difficult for several reasons.

• The states had little experience working together.

• The new nation lacked an army.

• The state militias that existed were poorly trained.

• The Continental Congress could not control counterfeiting, and thus could not maintain a stable economy.

To fight a war against the British successfully, the states had to work together. To do so successfully, they had to establish their own governments.

Creating State Governments. By 1780, most states had adopted written constitutions. These documents set forth the laws and principles of their governments. Some states simply revised their colonial **charters**. Others, such as Massachusetts, wrote new constitutions, which voters approved.

Despite differences among the new state constitutions, they shared certain features.

- The constitutions clearly spelled out the rights of citizens.

- Seven of the 13 documents contained a bill of rights.

- All of the state constitutions agreed that government existed only with the consent of the governed.

- The constitutions provided a separation of powers.

- Each state had an elected **legislature**.

- Most states had a **bicameral** legislature, consisting of a senate and a house of representatives.

- All states except Pennsylvania had a governor who enforced the laws.

Establishing a National Government. While the states were forming their governments, the Second Continental Congress began to write a constitution for the nation as a whole. In 1776 most Americans felt greater loyalty to their states than to the new nation. Although most people agreed that a national government was needed, they were unwilling to grant it too much power.

After many debates, the delegates finally agreed on a plan of government. The first constitution proposed to guide the United States government, completed in 1777, was called the Articles of Confederation.

The provisions of the Articles of Confederation stated that:

- Congress would be the national governing body.

- Congress had the power to declare war.

- Congress had the power to sign treaties with other nations.

- Delegates from each state would represent their states in Congress.

- Each state would have an equal vote in Congress.

Restrictions on the National Government

The Articles of Confederation established a national government that enabled the Americans to carry out their military campaign against Britain. But, fearing the abuses of power, the writers of the Articles intentionally limited the authority of the new government.

Power to Pass Laws. Although Congress had the power to make laws, at least 9 of the 13 states had to approve a law before it went into effect. The objections of only a few states could prevent important legislation from being enacted. Moreover, reaching agreements among the states was very difficult and took a long time. The states were often distrustful of one another, fearing that their interests might be in conflict.

Power to Tax. Congress did not have the power to **levy** taxes. It could raise money only by borrowing or by asking the states for funds.

charter *legal document issued by governments to define the purpose and privileges of corporations*

legislature *government agency responsible for making laws*

bicameral *consisting of two legislative chambers*

PRIMARY SOURCES

"I am mortified beyond expression that in the moment of our acknowledged independence we should by our conduct . . . render ourselves ridiculous . . . in the eyes of all Europe. We are fast verging to anarchy and confusion."
—*George Washington*

levy *to impose or collect by legal authority*

Furthermore, since the states were often unwilling to **levy** taxes against their citizens, money was in short supply. Congress did not even have the funds to pay its army officers.

Power to Regulate Trade. Congress did not have the power to regulate trade between the states. The states often acted independently of one another, sometimes imposing **tariffs** on goods imported from neighboring states. These tariffs were kept high to protect merchants and farmers from competitors in other states. As a result of such policies, trade relations between the states were often strained.

tariff *charge or tax placed on certain imported goods by a government*

A Call for Revision

revenue *income produced from a particular source*

The government's inability to raise needed tax **revenues** and to resolve continuing trade disputes between the states led many Americans to question the value of the Articles of Confederation. The national government's lack of authority was made still more evident when rebellion erupted in Massachusetts in 1786.

The Impact of Shays' Rebellion. During the American Revolution, many farmers left their land to fight the British. The task of producing the nation's food was left in the hands of fewer people, which led to reduced production, greater demand, and higher prices. To meet the demand, farmers borrowed money from banks for land, seed, animals, and tools. Since farm prices were up, banks were willing to lend money. When the war ended, however, crop prices dropped and many farmers were unable to repay the money they had borrowed.

Shays' Rebellion convinced many Americans that the Articles of Confederation were too weak to keep the new republic unified.

Farmers in western Massachusetts were especially hard hit by falling farm prices. To make matters worse, Massachusetts raised taxes. Many farmers were left with more debt than they could manage, and closed the courts to prevent judges from foreclosing on mortgages.

Daniel Shays was a Massachusetts farmer who had fought in the Revolution. In 1786 Shays gathered a force of 2,000 angry farmers, who attacked courthouses and tried to take a warehouse full of rifles and gunpowder. Massachusetts officials quickly raised an army and ended the rebellion.

Although Shays' Rebellion ended, many American leaders worried about the implications of the event. George Washington and other respected leaders feared that the Articles had given the national government too little power, rendering it incapable of maintaining order in the land. Only five years after the states had approved the Articles of Confederation, many Americans were calling for them to be changed.

Plans to Revise the Articles. Although Americans feared a strong national government, many leaders came to realize that a weak national government was just as dangerous. Even before Shays' Rebellion, several political leaders had openly begun to question the effectiveness of the Articles of Confederation. After Shays' Rebellion, leaders from several states called for a convention to "fix" the national government.

SECTION

3 Review

1. Defining Constitutional Terms

Write a brief definition for each of the following terms.

a. militia _____

b. charter _____

c. legislature _____

d. tariff _____

e. revenue _____

2. Reviewing Social Studies Skills: Using a Primary Source

Read the quotation below, which was written by George Washington in 1780. Do these words suggest that Washington favored or opposed a strong central government? Write a paragraph to explain your answer.

"I see one head gradually changing into 13. . . . I see the powers of Congress declining too fast for the consequence and respect which is due to them as a good representative body of America."

3. Reviewing the Main Ideas

Using complete sentences, answer each of the following questions.

a. What issues did Americans face after they declared their independence from Britain? _____

_____

_____

_____

_____

b. List three ways in which the Articles of Confederation weakened the new national government.

_____

_____

_____

_____

c. How did Shays' Rebellion change people's opinions about the Articles of Confederation? _____

_____

_____

_____

_____

4. Critical Thinking Skills: Understanding the Constitution

On a separate sheet of paper, write a paragraph to answer the following question.

Why do you think the Articles of Confederation were more successful during the Revolutionary War than they were after the war ended?

You Are the Judge

Hazelwood School District v. Kuhlmeier

The Issue: Freedom of the Press

Are students protected by the First Amendment right to free expression? In October 1987 the U.S. Supreme Court heard arguments in a case that decided whether student reporters are protected by the same First Amendment rights as are adult reporters. The case, *Hazelwood School District* v. *Kuhlmeier,* involved the principal and three student reporters from Hazelwood East High School, in Hazelwood, Missouri.

A Special Edition of the Spectrum

In 1983 Cathy Kuhlmeier, Leslie Smart, and Leanne Tippet were reporters for the *Spectrum,* Hazelwood East's weekly student newspaper. In May of that year the three students devoted a two-page special section of the *Spectrum* to articles on problems facing high school students. Issues such as parental divorce, teenage pregnancy, and runaway teens were featured.

The stories were researched and written entirely by the students and submitted by their journalism teacher to the school principal. Nothing in the stories was sexually explicit. Names were changed to protect the identity of the pregnant girls who were interviewed for the story.

Dr. Reynolds Responds

The *Spectrum* already had a reputation for publishing controversial articles, and Hazelwood's principal, Dr. Robert Reynolds, kept a close watch on the kinds of articles students were writing. When Dr. Reynolds read early versions of some of the articles scheduled for the May issue, he decided they were too controversial.

One story was about a student whose family was going through a painful divorce. The reporter interviewed a student who explained her views of the causes of her parents' problems. Although the reporter had removed the student's name from the final version of the story, her name appeared in the earlier version that the principal read. Dr. Reynolds felt that the story was an invasion of the student's and her family's privacy. Dr. Reynolds also objected to a story about three pregnant Hazelwood students. He thought that the story presented teenage pregnancy in a positive light and, therefore, would not permit its publication. The students working on the newspaper had written other articles for the special section discussing the difficulties of teen pregnancy. One article discussed the high failure rate of teenage marriages. Still, Dr. Reynolds felt that the material was inappropriate. He decided that the entire two-page supplement should not be published. Thus, when the May issue of *Spectrum* came out, none of the articles on teenage problems appeared.

The Students Respond

Believing that their First Amendment rights of free speech and press had been violated, the three reporters—Kuhlmeier, Smart, and Tippett—filed a lawsuit in 1983 against their principal. They claimed that the *Spectrum* was a public forum—a place where people could express their views freely.

The first court to hear the case, the U.S. District Court in St. Louis, ruled in 1985 that the principal and the school had a right to control what was published in the school newspaper. The court explained that the *Spectrum* was part of the school curriculum and that journalism students received course credit for their work. The principal, then, was exercising his responsibility for the students' education.

Exercising their constitutional right to appeal a court's verdict, the student reporters asked the U.S. Court of Appeals in 1985 to reconsider the case. In July 1986 the Court of Appeals overturned the lower district court ruling. Two of the three justices agreed with the students that the *Spectrum* was a public forum. As such, the student newspaper was protected by the First Amendment.

The Hazelwood School District then appealed the case to the U.S. Supreme Court. On October 13, 1987, the Supreme Court heard arguments from both sides in the dispute.

Arguments for the School District

1. The school district had the right to control a student newspaper published with the public's money if the school had a stated policy to do so.

2. The district should have broad control over the newspaper's content because it was part of the journalism curriculum. Students wrote articles for academic credit in a course.

Arguments for the Student Reporters

1. The *Spectrum* is a public forum and as such is protected by the First Amendment right to freedom of expression.

2. Public school officials should not be able to censor school-financed newspapers simply because they disagree with the paper's viewpoint.

Conclusion

In January 1988 the Supreme Court issued a ruling in this case. What are the constitutional and legal issues raised by this case? Suppose you were writing the Court's opinion. In whose favor would you decide— for the school district or for the student reporters?

CHAPTER 2

The Constitutional Convention

Ringing the Liberty Bell.

About This Chapter

On February 21, 1787, aware of its growing inability to deal with national issues, the Congress of the Confederation called on the states to send delegates to a national convention. The purpose of this meeting was to revise the Articles of Confederation in the hope of producing a more effective national government.

Soon after arriving in Philadelphia, the delegates (some of the most remarkable and distinguished citizens of the day) decided to dispense with the Articles entirely. They set about to draft a completely new constitution. After four months of debate, disagreement, and compromise, they presented the nation with a bold, new constitution. Despite its modest appearance—only 23 clauses—the document proved to be the blueprint for an enduring system of government. The delegates' next job was to persuade a strong and suspicious opposition to agree on the new constitution.

Delegates Meet in Philadelphia

As you read, think about the answers to these questions:

➤ Who attended the Constitutional Convention?

➤ What were the delegates like as a group?

➤ Who did not attend the Constitutional Convention and why?

➤ Who were some of the most important people at the convention?

The states responded quickly to the call to send representatives to a convention for the purpose of revising the Articles of Confederation. During the spring of 1787, state legislatures chose 74 delegates to attend this meeting. Of that number, 55 eventually participated in what we now call the Constitutional Convention, but what was then known as the Federal Convention. Only Rhode Island, whose political leaders were opposed to any strengthening of the national government, refused to send any delegates.

convention *gathering of persons for a common purpose*

delegate *person who is authorized to act as a representative for others*

Profile of the Delegates

Much has been written about the remarkable collection of individuals who gathered in Philadelphia in the summer of 1787. Thomas Jefferson later referred to the delegates as "an assembly of demigods." By this phrase he meant to emphasize their uncommon talent and intelligence, far from typical of the nearly 4 million Americans they represented. In the late 1700s, the vast majority of Americans lived and worked on small farms. By contrast, the delegates were largely wealthy and well educated.

demigod *person of such outstanding qualities as to be almost godlike*

Experience and Education. The delegates to the convention were among the most learned and politically experienced men of their time.

- 8 had signed the Declaration of Independence.
- 30 had served in the Continental Army.
- 6 had signed the Articles of Confederation.
- 8 had served in constitutional conventions in their own states.
- 7 had been or were still state governors.
- 39 had been members of the Continental Congress, the Congress of the Confederation, or both.

- 31 had attended college (at a time when few Americans received an education).

Age and Occupation.
Considering their experience, one of the most striking characteristics of the delegates was their youth. Only four delegates were over 60 years old, nearly half were in their 30s, and five were less than 30. Even when Benjamin Franklin's age of 81 is taken into account, the average age of the delegates was a mere 42.

Although the Framers represented a variety of occupations, more than half were lawyers, and many of those had held public office. Merchants and plantation owners made up the largest percentage of the remaining delegates. There were three doctors, two college presidents, and three college professors.

Who Was Missing

The term "Founding Fathers," which is used to refer to the convention delegates, immediately suggests one significant group that was missing from the famous gathering in Philadelphia. No women, blacks, or Native Americans participated in the Constitutional Convention. White men of modest means, who constituted 85% of the population, were represented by just two delegates of the same social standing.

Groups Not Represented.
While the absence of these groups might seem strange to us today, the delegates would have been equally surprised by the suggestion that they be allowed to participate. Despite the example of such remarkable and accomplished women as Abigail Adams (wife of John Adams) and Mercy Otis Warren (playwright and historian), women were viewed as dependents of their fathers or husbands. When they married, all that they owned became their husbands' property. They could neither vote nor hold office.

Free blacks and Native Americans also lacked political and legal rights. Even white men without property could not hold political office. Many poor and middle-class whites could not vote for the same reason.

Advocates of States' Rights.
Some of the strongest supporters of the rights of the states were missing from the convention. Patrick Henry of Virginia, famous for his fierce devotion to liberty, decided early on to stay home, saying that he "smelt a rat." In other words, he believed that the convention's planners might be using the meeting to establish a powerful central government. Other prominent citizens—Samuel Adams of Massachusetts, Governor George Clinton of New York, and Samuel Chase of Maryland—were not selected as delegates by their states. Rhode Island boycotted the convention entirely, thus giving up any influence it might have had on the final outcome.

Several Prominent Americans.
Several of the better-known leaders of the Revolutionary period were also missing from Philadelphia.

- Thomas Jefferson, author of the Declaration of Independence, was in Paris at the time, serving as minister to France.

boycott *to avoid using, buying, or dealing with as a means of protest*

- John Adams, envoy to England and Holland, was also out of the country.

- Thomas Paine was in Europe trying to promote his recently invented design for an iron bridge.

Jefferson and Adams managed to influence some of the proceedings through letters and a book about constitutions that Adams had just published.

Key Delegates

Some of the delegates who attended the convention in Philadelphia played more significant roles than others in the process of writing the Constitution.

George Washington. Although Washington had retired to his Mt. Vernon estate at the end of the Revolutionary War, he was still one of the best known and most respected men in America. His decision to attend the convention helped to attract other important individuals to Philadelphia. Washington rarely participated in the debates, but as president of the convention he guided the proceedings with a firm hand.

James Madison. Despite his unimpressive appearance, the 36-year-old Madison contributed more to the creation of the Constitution than any other individual—for which he became known as the "Father of the Constitution." Exceptionally well educated in history and government, he quickly became the convention's floor leader. Most of what is known of the proceedings is the result of his careful, detailed *Notes*.

Benjamin Franklin. Senior statesman of the convention, Franklin enjoyed an international reputation as a writer, scientist, inventor, and diplomat. Despite failing health that forced him to miss many of the convention's sessions, Franklin played an important role as conciliator during the often heated debates at the convention.

Gouverneur Morris. Only 35 at the time, Morris was disabled as a result of an accident. Even though he had a wooden leg and could not use one of his arms, he was an active participant at the convention, delivering even more speeches than Madison. Morris was a gifted writer and is given credit for most of the actual language in the Constitution.

Alexander Hamilton. A brilliant lawyer and influential figure in New York politics, the 32-year-old Hamilton had served as Washington's secretary during the Revolutionary War. Hamilton admired the British system of government and was probably the convention's most passionate advocate of a strong national government. His desire for a single chief executive, chosen for life, came close to a wish for monarchy.

PRIMARY SOURCES

"I consider the difference between a system founded on the legislatures only, and one founded on the people, to be the true difference between a league or treaty and a constitution."
—James Madison

conciliator *person who settles disputes or restores friendships*

Name _____ **Date** _____

1 Review

1. Defining Constitutional Terms

Write a brief definition for each of the following terms.

a. convention _____

b. delegate _____

c. boycott _____

d. envoy _____

e. conciliator _____

2. Reviewing Social Studies Skills: Reading for Historical Facts

Write the answer to each of the following questions in the space provided.

a. Where did the Constitutional Convention take place? _____

b. What was the Constitutional Convention known as in 1787? _____

c. Who was president of the Constitutional Convention? _____

3. Reviewing the Main Ideas

Using complete sentences, answer each of the following questions.

a. Why did Rhode Island refuse to send delegates to the Constitutional Convention? _____

_____

_____

_____

b. How did the delegates differ from typical Americans of their time? _____

_____

_____

_____

c. What people or groups did not participate in the convention? _____

_____

_____

_____

d. Who were some of the most important delegates at the convention? _____

_____

_____

_____

4. Critical Thinking Skills: Understanding the Constitution

On a separate sheet of paper, write a paragraph to answer the following question.

How might the Constitution have turned out differently if some of the groups missing from the convention had been represented in Philadelphia?

Convention Proceedings and Compromises

As you read, think about the answers to these questions:

➤ What decisions did the delegates make in the opening days of the Constitutional Convention?

➤ In what ways was the Virginia Plan different from the New Jersey Plan?

➤ Which of the compromises reached by the Constitutional Convention were most important?

➤ What steps did delegates take to finalize the Constitution?

The Convention Opens

The Constitutional Convention did not get off to a smooth start. Only a handful of delegates from two states showed up in the Pennsylvania State House for the convention's opening on May 14. Spring rains and muddy roads delayed the arrival of many of the delegates for days. A **quorum** was finally achieved on May 25, with 29 delegates from 7 states. By a unanimous vote, they elected George Washington president of the convention and adopted several rules of procedure.

The Need for Secrecy. The delegates decided that all debates and discussion should be kept secret. The convention had already attracted much public attention, and the delegates hoped to protect themselves from outside pressure and ensure that they could speak their minds freely. To enforce secrecy, guards were placed outside the doors of the State House.

Deciding to Write a New Constitution. The convention had been called "for the sole and express purpose of revising the Articles of Confederation," and the delegates shared a strong sense of urgency about the task ahead of them. It was clear that the Articles did not give the government the power it needed to resolve disputes and misunderstanding that had arisen between states.

Even before the meeting began, however, several delegates believed that more was needed than a simple revision of the Articles. James Madison already had an outline for a new constitution and Alexander Hamilton declared that the Articles "are fit neither for war nor peace." Just five days into the convention, the delegates adopted a proposal to write a completely new constitution.

quorum *minimum number of members who must be present for the valid transaction of business*

PRIMARY SOURCES

"My wish is that the Convention may probe the defects of the [Articles] to the bottom, and provide radical cures."
—George Washington

The Virginia and New Jersey Plans

In the early weeks of the convention, the delegates spent much of their time debating the merits of two very different plans for the structure of a new government.

The Virginia Plan. The first plan, proposed by Edmund Randolph of Virginia and written largely by James Madison, was known as the Virginia Plan. It included several major proposals:

- The federal government would have three separate branches—**legislative**, **executive**, and **judicial**.

- Congress (the national **legislature**) would consist of two houses: the House of Representatives and the Senate.

- In both houses, the number of representatives from each state would be based on its population.

- Voters in each state would elect the members of the House of Representatives who, in turn, would choose the members of the Senate from lists of people nominated by state legislatures.

- Congress would have all the powers it held under the Articles of Confederation plus the power to make laws for the states, to override state laws, and to force states to obey national laws.

- Congress would choose members of the judicial branch as well as a President.

Those who feared a strong central government objected to the Virginia Plan because it gave Congress too much authority over state legislatures. The main protests came from smaller states, such as New Jersey and Delaware, which had smaller populations and would, therefore, have fewer representatives in Congress under this plan.

The New Jersey Plan. After two weeks of intense debate, William Paterson of New Jersey proposed the alternative known as the New Jersey Plan. Paterson's plan also called for three branches of government and granted the government more powers than the Articles of Confederation had. The New Jersey Plan, however, differed in several important ways.

- All states, large or small, would have an equal number of representatives in Congress (just as they had under the Articles).

- Congress would consist of only one house, to be elected by the state legislatures rather than directly by the people.

- Congress would choose several people to serve in the executive branch. These people would, in turn, have the power to appoint members of the judicial branch.

On the whole, the New Jersey Plan retained the major features of the Articles of Confederation. The Virginia Plan, on the other hand, called for a new and more powerful national government. The delegates argued over these two plans for weeks. At times the debate grew so intense that several delegates on both sides threatened to walk out. For a while it looked as if the conflict would destroy the convention.

legislative *having the power to make laws*

executive *having the power to carry out laws*

judicial *having the power to tell what laws mean and decide if they are carried out fairly*

legislature *lawmaking body*

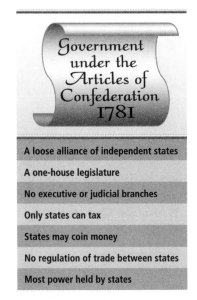

Government under the Articles of Confederation 1781

A loose alliance of independent states

A one-house legislature

No executive or judicial branches

Only states can tax

States may coin money

No regulation of trade between states

Most power held by states

Without some form of centralized leadership and authority, the new government would have been powerless to deal with the unpredictable behavior of the states.

Independence Hall was the site of many vigorous debates as each delegate sought to make sure his own state's interests were protected. Ultimately, compromise was key to the convention's success.

Compromises Get the Job Done

Although the Framers debated many critical points, they also agreed on several basic issues. They were all dedicated to the concepts of **popular sovereignty** and limited national government. Most supported a representative system of government and separate branches of government that curbed each other's power through a system of checks and balances. Yet their disputes were still serious and threatened to disrupt the convention on several occasions. In the end, the Constitution was born out of a series of creative **compromises**.

popular sovereignty *self-government based on the will of the people*

The Great Compromise. Just when it seemed that the debate over the Virginia and New Jersey Plans would bring the convention to an end, Roger Sherman of Connecticut proposed a compromise to the delegates. The Great Compromise, which was also known as the Connecticut Compromise, proposed that:

compromise *settlement of differences in which each side gives up something*

- Congress should consist of two houses, a House of Representatives and a Senate.
- A state's representation in the House would be based on population.
- Each state would have two representatives in the Senate.

On July 16 the delegates accepted Sherman's plan by a narrow margin and opened the door for the delegates to compromise on other issues.

The Three-Fifths Compromise. The next major issue facing the convention split the delegates from the northern and southern states. Southerners, who wanted to increase their representation in the House, wanted their slaves counted as population. Northerners protested, arguing that since slaves could not vote, they should not be counted.

After long and bitter dispute, another compromise was reached. The delegates agreed that three fifths of the slaves in any state would be counted in population figures—both for representation and for taxation.

Today the Three-Fifths Compromise is troubling to most people. It suggests that the Framers approved of slavery and that they seemed to be saying that a black person was worth only three-fifths as much as a white person. In fact, many of the Framers disapproved of slavery. They knew, however, that they needed to accept this compromise in order to ensure

The work of the delegates is reflected in this woodcut symbolizing the blessings of liberty and the rule of law.

PRIMARY SOURCES

"Mr. President, I confess that there are several parts of this Constitution which I do not at present approve, but . . . the older I grow, the more apt I am to doubt my own judgment, and to pay more respect to the judgment of others. . . . In these sentiments, Sir, I agree to this Constitution with all its faults . . ."
—Benjamin Franklin

resolution *statement of a group's opinion or decision*

clause *section of a document*

the survival of the new federal government. The compromise was removed from the Constitution in 1865, when slavery was abolished by the 13th Amendment.

Commerce and Slave Trade Agreements. Delegates who favored a strong central government wanted the new Congress to control trade between the states and foreign countries. But the South's agricultural economy depended heavily on exports, and southern delegates insisted that Congress be forbidden to tax the exports of any state. Southerners also argued that the slave trade was crucial to their region's economy. But many northerners wanted to abolish it completely. Once again the delegates reached a compromise, whereby Congress could not interfere with the slave trade for at least 20 years after the Constitution went into effect.

The Convention Completes Its Work

As compromises were made and agreements were reached, the delegates took several steps to complete their work.

- They formed the Committee of Detail to assemble all the **resolutions** they had passed.

- They appointed Gouverneur Morris to head the Committee on Style, which revised the Constitution's language into its final form.

- They assembled in the State House on September 17, 1787, to sign their names to the Constitution—a document of 23 **clauses** that changed American history.

Few delegates were completely happy with the document. Nevertheless, the Framers agreed to go forward and present it to the public.

Name _____ Date _____

2 Review

1. Defining Constitutional Terms
Write a brief definition for each of the following terms.

a. quorum _____

b. legislative _____

c. executive _____

d. judicial _____

e. popular sovereignty _____

f. compromise _____

g. resolution _____

h. clause _____

2. Reviewing Social Studies Skills: Sequencing Events
Rewrite the following list of events in chronological order.

Three-Fifths Compromise is reached.	1. _____
Delegates sign the Constitution.	2. _____
New Jersey Plan is introduced.	3. _____
Delegates decide to write a new Constitution.	4. _____
Virginia Plan is introduced.	5. _____
Great Compromise is reached.	6. _____

3. Reviewing the Main Ideas
Using complete sentences, answer the following questions.

a. What important decisions did the delegates reach in the first days of the convention? _____

_____

_____

b. In what ways were the Virginia and New Jersey Plans similar and different? _____

_____

c. What compromises were most crucial to the success of the convention? _____

_____

d. What did the delegates do to complete the process of writing the Constitution? _____

_____

_____

4. Critical Thinking Skills: Understanding the Constitution
On a separate piece of paper, write a paragraph to answer the following question.

How would the Constitution and the system of government it created have been different if they had been based on the New Jersey Plan?

As you read, think about the answers to these questions:

➤ How did the Federalists and Antifederalists view the new Constitution?

➤ Which states had the strongest opposition to the Constitution?

➤ What were the first acts of the new government?

Drawing the Battle Lines

ratify *to give formal approval*

censure *to express disapproval*

The delegates in Philadelphia knew that ratifying the new Constitution would be difficult. A group of representatives wanted to censure the convention for going beyond their instructions to revise the Articles of Confederation. The motion was defeated, however, and on September 28, Congress submitted the new document to the states for their consideration.

Procedures. Anticipating the strong opposition to the new Constitution, the Framers set up a process that would improve its chances of ratification.

- They recommended that the document be sent to state constitutional conventions for approval rather than to state legislatures.

- The voters in each state would elect representatives to serve in these special conventions.

Delegates gathered in the State House on September 7, 1787, to sign their names to the document they had labored so hard to create.

- In this way, the people would decide the fate of the Constitution instead of state officials, who had an interest in keeping power for themselves.

- Article VII of the Constitution specified that only nine states were needed for ratification, which greatly improved the odds of its gaining approval.

The Federalists. As soon as the Constitutional Convention had ended, the delegates went to work to ensure the ratification of the document they had

worked so hard to produce. Those who supported the Constitution became known as Federalists (because of their desire for a strong national government). They emphasized the weaknesses of the Articles of Confederation and argued that only a new government based on the proposed Constitution would have the authority to solve the new nation's problems.

Among the most active and influential of the Federalists were James Madison, Alexander Hamilton, and John Jay. They wrote a series of essays that were published in newspapers in New York City. These 85 essays, known as the *Federalist Papers,* answered the objections of those who opposed the Constitution—the Antifederalists.

The Antifederalists. Opponents of the Constitution, who were known as Antifederalists, objected to the Constitution for many reasons.

- The document made the national government too strong and gave the President too much power.

- The indirect method of electing the President and Senate removed government too far from the people.

- The ratification process was unsatisfactory.

- The document lacked a bill of rights to protect citizens' individual liberties.

- Small states feared that they would be dominated by large ones.

Ratifying the Constitution

Delaware was the first state to ratify the Constitution on December 7, 1787. Pennsylvania, New Jersey, Georgia, and Connecticut followed within several weeks. In Massachusetts, a stronghold of Antifederalist sentiment, the delegates were more evenly divided. After a heated debate, the state convention finally ratified the Constitution in February 1788, by a vote of 187 to 168. Maryland and South Carolina soon followed.

In June, New Hampshire became the ninth state to approve the blueprint for a new government. Although technically the Constitution could have gone into effect at that point, Virginia and New York had not yet voted to ratify. Without the approval of these two large and important states, the new government could not hope to succeed.

For the Constitution to become law, ratification by nine states was needed.

Ratification of the Constitution

State	Date	Vote
Delaware	December 7, 1787	30–0
Pennsylvania	December 12, 1787	46–23
New Jersey	December 18, 1787	38–0
Georgia	January 2, 1788	26–0
Connecticut	January 9, 1788	128–40
Massachusetts	February 6, 1788	187–168
Maryland	April 28, 1788	63–11
South Carolina	May 23, 1788	149–73
New Hampshire	June 21, 1788	57–47
Virginia	June 25, 1788	89–79
New York	July 26, 1788	30–27
North Carolina	November 21, 1789*	194–77
Rhode Island	May 29, 1790	34–32

*Second vote; ratification was originally defeated on August 4, 1788, by a vote of 184–84.

Virginia and New York. Virginia delegates James Madison and Edmund Randolph had played a crucial role in creating the Constitution. Yet among those opposed to ratification were such well-known and respected Virginia politicians as Patrick Henry, George Mason, and Richard Henry Lee. They worried that the Constitution lacked sufficient safeguards to protect the individual liberties of the people.

dissent *to disagree or withhold approval*

successor *person or thing that replaces or follows another*

Although George Washington was not a delegate to the ratifying convention, his strong support for ratification proved decisive. Together with Madison, he was able to persuade several other wavering delegates. Even so, the vote for approval was close—89 to 79.

When the New York convention first assembled, fully two thirds of the delegates, led by Antifederalist Governor George Clinton, opposed the Constitution. Fortunately, Hamilton and other supporters were able to delay the convention's final vote for several weeks. News of the votes in New Hampshire and Virginia also helped the Federalist cause. On July 26, New York ratified the Constitution by the narrow margin of only three votes.

Although Rhode Island and North Carolina initially rejected the Constitution, the support of Virginia and New York guaranteed the future of the new government. The two dissenting states finally ratified—but only after the new government had begun operations.

Call for a Bill of Rights. When Massachusetts ratified the Constitution, the state convention proposed a series of amendments that would guarantee the rights of citizens. Several other states—including Virginia, New Hampshire, and South Carolina—based their approval of the Constitution on the condition that a bill of rights be added.

Without the promise of an addition of a bill of rights, it is possible that the Federalists might have failed in their fight for ratification.

Forming a New Government

On September 13, 1788, in its last act under the Articles, the Congress of the Confederation paved the way for its successor. It chose New York City as the temporary capital and set a date in January for selecting presidential electors.

Choosing a President and Congress. On February 4, electors voted for President and Vice President. On March 4, the new Congress met in Federal Hall on Wall Street. Because it lacked a quorum, the votes could not be counted until April 6. George Washington had been elected President and John Adams, Vice President. Three weeks later, Washington took the oath of office as the first President of the United States.

Drafting and Ratifying the Bill of Rights. Many of the states had ratified the Constitution with the understanding that a bill of rights would be added. The First Congress, consisting of 59 representatives and 26 senators, approved a series of 12 amendments in 1789. Written by James Madison, 10 of these amendments were ratified in 1791 and came to be known collectively as the Bill of Rights. One of the two remaining amendments proposed by Madison was finally ratified in 1992, becoming the 27th Amendment.

SECTION

3 Review

1. Defining Constitutional Terms
Write a brief definition for each of the following terms.

a. ratify _____

b. censure _____

c. dissent _____

d. successor _____

2. Reviewing Social Studies Skills: Finding Evidence
To respond to the following questions, write the *exact* sentence from the lesson that contains the answer.

a. Why did some of the delegates want to censure the convention? _____

_____

b. Which three influential Virginians were opposed to the Constitution? _____

_____

_____

c. Why did the Massachusetts ratifying convention propose that a bill of rights be added to the Constitution?

_____

_____

3. Reviewing the Main Ideas
Using complete sentences, answer the following questions.

a. What was the difference between the Federalists' and Antifederalists' positions on the new Constitution?

_____

_____

b. Why was the support of New York and Virginia so important, even after nine states had ratified the Constitution?

_____

_____

c. What important action did the First Congress take in 1789? _____

_____

_____

4. Critical Thinking Skills: Understanding the Constitution
On a separate sheet of paper, write a paragraph to answer the following question.

Why did the promise of a bill of rights convince many delegates at state ratifying conventions to vote in favor of the Constitution?

You Are the Judge

New Jersey v. T.L.O.

Setting the Scene:

You are in your gym locker room with a friend. As you change into your street clothes, your friend lights up a cigarette and begins to smoke. You hear the gym teacher heading your way. Knowing he'll smell the smoke as soon as he walks by, your friend throws the cigarette into a wastebasket. The gym teacher accuses both of you of smoking and takes you to the principal's office. The principal demands that you empty your pockets and your backpack to prove you were not smoking. Is this fair? More important, is it legal?

The Issue: Search and Seizure

Should school officials be required to have a warrant to search a student's property in a public school? In 1985 the Supreme Court confronted this question of the constitutional protection against search and seizure, guaranteed by the Fourth Amendment. That year it heard a case involving the search of a girl's purse in school.

Searching Her Purse

In 1980 a teacher caught two 14-year-old girls smoking in a washroom at Piscataway High School in New Jersey. It was against school rules for students to smoke on school grounds. The principal talked to both girls. One admitted smoking; the other said she never smoked.

The principal took the second girl to his office. Because she was a minor, the girl was referred to as T.L.O.—her initials—to keep her identity secret. The principal searched T.L.O.'s purse, where he found cigarette rolling papers. The principal thought that having cigarette papers might indicate the use of marijuana. Searching further, he found a small amount of marijuana, a pipe, and several empty plastic bags. Other items in T.L.O.'s purse revealed that she might have been selling drugs to students.

The police and T.L.O.'s mother were notified. The police took T.L.O. and the evidence to police headquarters, where she confessed to selling marijuana to other students. In juvenile court T.L.O. was declared a delinquent on the evidence found in her purse and her confession. She received a year's probation, or a suspended sentence, as punishment.

T.L.O. appealed her case to the Superior Court of New Jersey. Her lawyer argued that the contents of T.L.O.'s purse should not have been presented as evidence in court. He cited the Fourth Amendment to the U.S. Constitution, which states that a warrant must be obtained before searching an individual's property. The principal had not obtained such a warrant before he searched T.L.O.'s purse.

Appealing to the U.S. Supreme Court

The Superior Court of New Jersey upheld the juvenile court's decision to admit the evidence. T.L.O.

then appealed to the Supreme Court of New Jersey, which reversed the lower court ruling. The New Jersey Supreme Court ruled that the evidence should not have been admitted because T.L.O.'s Fourth Amendment rights had been violated; the evidence had been illegally obtained. The State of New Jersey then appealed to the U.S. Supreme Court.

Review the following evidence and arguments presented to the U.S. Supreme Court:

New Jersey's Arguments in Favor of Admitting the Evidence

1. School officials are not the police. They should not have to operate under the same restraints as police.

2. Teachers and principals are acting for the parents of the students. Parents do not need a warrant to search their children.

3. Schools must make the school environment one in which young people can learn. School officials need broad powers of discipline and action to do this.

4. The teacher caught the students in the act of breaking a school rule. One girl admitted breaking a rule. T.L.O. was suspected of breaking the same rule, so the principal was justified in searching her possessions. He had good reason to suspect that she broke a school rule. When he found the marijuana papers, he also had good reason to suspect that she had broken a law.

T.L.O.'s Lawyer's Arguments Against Admitting the Evidence

1. Students are entitled to the protection of the U.S. Constitution. Since the principal did not have a warrant to search T.L.O., the evidence found should not have been used against her.

2. The teachers and the principal were government agents and employees of the State of New Jersey. They were not acting as the student's parents who do have the right to search the students.

3. Students have a right to personal privacy in school.

4. The principal did not have a good reason to search T.L.O., so anything he found should not have been used against her.

Conclusion

The Supreme Court issued its ruling in this case in 1985. What constitutional and legal issues are raised by this case? Suppose you were writing the Court's opinion. In whose favor would you decide—T.L.O.'s or the State of New Jersey's? What might change your answer? What if someone told your teacher that you had a gun in your locker? Could the teacher search your locker? What if the teacher wanted to search for something banned from school, but not otherwise illegal, such as a cell phone?

3 An Enduring Document

Viewing the Constitution at the National Archives in Washington, D.C.

About This Chapter

The United States Constitution, in its original form, contains fewer than 5,000 words. Dealing with basic principles, its sections are often brief and lacking in detail. As the Framers intended, it is open to interpretation and change. To ensure that the Constitution would meet the needs of a growing society, the Framers created a formal way to change the Constitution. In addition, an informal process of change—through custom and interpretation—has also helped to keep the Constitution relevant and flexible for more than 200 years. President Woodrow Wilson once observed that the Constitution in action is "a very different thing from the Constitution of the books."

SECTION 1

Constitutional Principles

As you read, think about the answers to these questions:

➤ According to the Constitution, what is the source of the government's authority?

➤ What does the concept of limited government mean?

➤ How does the federal system divide governmental powers?

➤ What is the purpose of separation of powers?

➤ Whose power is limited by the system of checks and balances?

Despite many conflicts and disagreements, the Constitutional Convention delegates shared a belief in certain principles of government—principles that reflect some of the fundamental values of our democratic system.

Popular Sovereignty

The first principle underlying the Constitution is that of popular sovereignty. Expressed in the opening words of the Constitution: "We, the people . . . ," the Framers of the Constitution made it clear that the power and authority of the government comes from the American people. Although revolutionary at the time, this idea lies at the heart of all democracies today.

Limiting the Power of Government

Remembering the struggles against British tyranny, the Framers wanted to create a government that would be effective but not too powerful. Consequently, they included in their plan the concept of limited government, which means that

- The national government does not have absolute authority,
- The government may do only those things that the people have given it the power to do,
- Government must obey its own laws, and
- Government must be conducted according to constitutional principles.

> **PRIMARY SOURCES**
>
> *"The powers not delegated to the United States by the Constitution, nor prohibited by it to the states, are reserved to the states respectively, or to the people."*
> —Amendment 10 of the U.S. Constitution

tyranny *government in which a single person has complete power*

limited government *idea that government is limited in what it may do and each citizen has certain rights that cannot be taken away*

constitutionalism *principle that government and its officials are bound by fundamental law*

rule of law *refers to constitutionalism, the principle that government is bound by fundamental law*

federalism *system of government in which power is divided between the national and state governments*

For these reasons, limited government has also been called constitutionalism and rule of law. This means that government and its officers are always subject to the law, never above it.

Sharing of Power

Under the Constitution, the states had to give up some of their powers to the new federal government. The division of powers between national and state governments is called federalism. The federal system enables the national government to act for the nation as a whole, while granting authority to the states to deal with local issues.

What the Federal Government Can Do. The Constitution carefully lists the powers of the federal government. These include the power to coin money, regulate trade between states and foreign countries, establish a postal system, create and maintain armed forces, conduct foreign policy, and declare war. The Framers also gave Congress the power to "make all laws which shall be necessary and proper for carrying into execution the foregoing powers . . ." This so-called elastic clause gives Congress flexibility in dealing with the changing needs of the nation.

elastic clause *constitutional power that gives Congress the authority to make the laws needed to carry out its other responsibilities*

What State Governments Can Do. The Constitution reserves to state governments the power to establish qualifications for voting, conduct elections, regulate trade within their borders, create local governments, and establish and maintain schools. Apart from the powers just listed, the states exercise many undefined powers.

Shared Powers. Shared powers are those that the Constitution neither grants explicitly to the national government nor denies to the states. They include, for example, levying and collecting taxes and defining crimes. Because the Framers realized that the federal and state governments would sometimes disagree about who had authority in certain areas, they made the Constitution, and the laws made in support of it, the "supreme law of the land."

Separation of Powers

The Framers further limited the federal government by dividing it into three independent branches: legislative, executive, and judicial. This system is referred to as a separation of powers.

separation of powers *duties and responsibilities of government are divided into three separate but co-equal branches: executive, legislative, and judicial*

Congress. Congress, which consists of the House of Representatives and the Senate, is the legislative branch. Article I of the Constitution grants Congress the power to collect taxes, regulate trade between nations and states, and declare war. Its main function is to make laws to carry out these and other powers listed in Article I.

The President. The executive branch of the government consists of the President, the Vice President, and a variety of departments and personnel. The President's primary role is to enforce the laws that Congress passes. The President, or the chief executive, serves as commander in chief of the armed forces. He (or she) can propose laws, appoint federal judges, and negotiate foreign trade agreements.

The Judiciary. The courts make up the judicial branch. Article III establishes a Supreme Court and gives Congress the power to set up lower federal courts. The primary function of the federal courts is to interpret the Constitution and the laws and to ensure that they are applied fairly. Federal courts also hear disputes between states.

Protecting Against Tyranny

The Framers established a system in which each branch of the government has some way to check, or control, the other two. Referred to as checks and balances, this system strengthens the separation of powers and further limits the authority of the federal government. It makes compromise a necessary and vital part of our system of government.

Checks by the Legislature. The Senate approves the President's choices for Cabinet officers, federal judges, and ambassadors. The Senate approves treaties that the President negotiates with foreign nations. Congress can override the President's veto of a bill. Congress may remove a President, Vice President, or federal judges from office through impeachment. Congress may propose amendments to the Constitution in an effort to override judicial decisions.

Checks by the Executive. The President may veto a bill passed by Congress, call special sessions, and recommend legislation.

Checks by the Judiciary. The Supreme Court has the power of judicial review. That means that it may declare a law or an executive action in violation of the Constitution, or unconstitutional. This power is not spelled out in the Constitution, but some of the Framers believed it to be a basic principle of American government.

Checking the Power of the People. Although the Framers feared a central government with too much power, they also worried that the people might abuse their power. The delegates believed that direct participation in the national government should be limited to the better educated and more privileged Americans. So they took steps to limit the power of the people. They decided that

- Voters would elect representatives directly.

- State legislatures would choose the senators from their state. (This method lasted until 1913, when Congress passed the 17th Amendment, allowing the people to elect their senators directly.)

- State legislatures would choose electors equal to the number of its representatives. Known collectively as the electoral college, the electors would choose the President and Vice President. (Since the mid-1800s, voters have chosen presidential electors directly, and these electors customarily follow the popular vote of their respective states.)

checks and balances *each branch of government is subject to certain restraints by the other two*

impeachment *act of accusing or formally charging with misconduct*

veto *to reject or prevent a bill from becoming law*

judicial review *power of the courts to determine whether legislative and executive actions are in accordance with the Constitution*

unconstitutional *in violation of the Constitution*

Name _____ Date _____

1. Defining Constitutional Terms

Write a brief definition for each of the following terms.

a. constitutionalism _____

b. federalism _____

c. elastic clause _____

d. judicial review _____

e. impeachment _____

f. unconstitutional _____

2. Reviewing Social Studies Skills: Organizing Facts

The six words below describe the powers delegated to the three branches of government. In the spaces provided, write the two words associated with each branch of government.

veto	interpret	impeach
review	appoint	override

a. Supreme Court _____

b. Congress _____

c. President _____

3. Reviewing the Main Ideas

Using complete sentences, answer each of the following questions.

a. In what sense is the Constitution a statement of limited government? _____

_____

b. Explain why the American system of government is an example of federalism. _____

_____

c. How does the system of checks and balances affect the way in which the government works? _____

_____

_____

d. How does the Supreme Court use judicial review to control the power of Congress and the President?

_____

_____

_____

4. Critical Thinking Skills: Understanding the Constitution

On a separate sheet of paper, write a paragraph to answer the following question.

The government of the United States is limited by federalism, separation of powers, and the system of checks and balances. How might our system of government and society be different without such limitations?

The Amendment Process

As you read, think about the answers to these questions:

➤ How can the Constitution be formally changed?

➤ What does the Bill of Rights protect?

➤ Which other amendments have had a significant impact on our system of government and on our lives?

The delegates in Philadelphia knew that the Constitution would need to adjust to times and conditions they couldn't possibly foresee. As a result, the Framers provided a formal procedure to **amend** the Constitution.

amend *to change or add to*

Changing the Constitution by Amendment

While recognizing the need for flexibility, the Framers wanted future generations to consider proposed changes carefully before amending the Constitution. To ensure that changes would not be made in haste, they created a complicated amendment process.

Proposing and Ratifying Amendments. Article V of the Constitution outlines two methods for proposing amendments.

PRIMARY SOURCES

"No society can make a perpetual constitution, or a perpetual law."
—*Thomas Jefferson*

• Two thirds of both houses of Congress can propose an amendment.

• A special national convention, called by Congress at the request of two thirds of the state legislatures, can propose an amendment.

The Constitution also provides two ways to ratify, or approve, proposed amendments. An amendment becomes part of the Constitution

• when it is approved by the legislatures in three fourths (currently 38) of the states;

• when it is approved by special ratifying conventions in three fourths of the states.

Although the Framers did not include a time limit for ratification, the Supreme Court has ruled that it must occur within "some reasonable time." Congress has defined that period as seven years. The Court, however, may grant extra time.

Amending the Constitution is not an easy process. It is difficult to win a two-thirds vote in one, let alone both, houses of Congress. Furthermore, if Congress succeeds in gathering the votes to propose an amendment, there is no guarantee that three quarters of the states will then ratify it.

joint resolution *act proposed by both houses of Congress and used to propose constitutional amendments*

Since 1789, members of Congress have formally proposed more than 10,000 **joint resolutions** calling for amendments. Congress has sent only 33 of these amendments to the states, and only 27 have been ratified. With remarkably few changes, the Constitution has shaped and guided our system of government for more than 200 years.

Guarantees of Basic Freedoms

Even as the states were debating whether to adopt the Constitution, many people worried about the government's power over its citizens. They did not want the government to repeat the abuses that they suffered as colonists under British rule.

One of the first acts of the new Congress was the passage of a series of amendments, which were ratified by the states in 1791. These ten amendments, known as the Bill of Rights, aim to protect Americans' basic freedoms against the power of the federal government.

PRIMARY SOURCES

"How will we be protected against unjust acts of government?"
—Patrick Henry

The Bill of Rights. The First Amendment protects the fundamental rights, or essential freedoms, of the people.

- The First Amendment prohibits the government from establishing a state church, supporting religious practices, or showing preference for one religion over another. It prohibits Congress from restricting freedom of religion, freedom of speech, freedom of assembly, and freedom of the press; and protects the right to petition the government to remove the cause of grievances.

The next three amendments grew out of the colonists' struggles against British tyranny.

- The Second Amendment guarantees the continued existence of state **militias**, thus ensuring the right of the people to bear arms.

militia *armed citizens who are called for service in times of emergency*

- The Third Amendment prohibits the government from forcing people to house soldiers in their homes, except according to law.

- The Fourth Amendment protects citizens against unreasonable searches and seizure of their property.

Amendments Five through Eight concern the rights of citizens who are accused of crimes.

due process *legal proceedings carried out according to established rules and principles*

- The Fifth Amendment guarantees **due process** of law when a person is accused and tried for a crime. It also says that people do not have to give evidence in court that might hurt them and that they cannot be tried twice for the same crime.

- The Sixth Amendment guarantees people a trial by jury in criminal cases and the right to a lawyer.

civil *relating to ordinary community life as opposed to criminal proceedings*

- The Seventh Amendment guarantees the right to a jury trial in **civil** cases involving more than $20.

bail *money given to secure the temporary release of an accused individual while he or she is awaiting trial*

- The Eighth Amendment prevents judges from setting excessive **bail** or handing out cruel and unusual punishments.

The last two amendments limit the powers of the federal government to those powers granted in the Constitution.

- The Ninth Amendment says that the rights of citizens are not limited to only those described in the Constitution.
- The Tenth Amendment grants that any powers not given in the Constitution to the federal government belong to the states.

Individual Rights Versus Majority Rule. The Bill of Rights is a powerful declaration of the rights of individuals. At the same time, the Constitution created a democracy based on the rule of the majority. According to majority rule, decisions are made by a majority vote, and the viewpoint of the minority is defeated. But when the will of the majority conflicts with individual liberties, which principle should be followed?

The Bill of Rights has been at the center of some of the most important and controversial Supreme Court cases in our country's history. In these cases the justices have had to struggle to find a balance between individual liberty and majority rule.

Other Amendments

The Framers made it so difficult to alter the Constitution that Congress and the states have done so only rarely. In the 200 years following the Bill of Rights, only 17 more amendments were ratified. The 11th Amendment concerns the immunity of the states from certain lawsuits, and the 12th Amendment consists of changes to the electoral college procedures.

The Civil War Amendments. Perhaps the most significant amendments ratified after the Bill of Rights are the three so-called Civil War amendments that were passed to protect the rights of former slaves. These measures were adopted shortly after the Civil War.

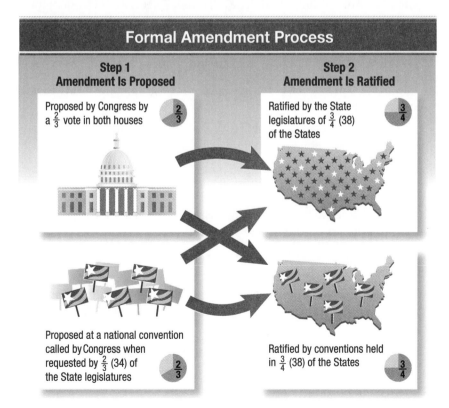

Formal Amendment Process

**Step 1
Amendment Is Proposed**

Proposed by Congress by a $\frac{2}{3}$ vote in both houses — $\frac{2}{3}$

Proposed at a national convention called by Congress when requested by $\frac{2}{3}$ (34) of the State legislatures — $\frac{2}{3}$

**Step 2
Amendment Is Ratified**

Ratified by the State legislatures of $\frac{3}{4}$ (38) of the States — $\frac{3}{4}$

Ratified by conventions held in $\frac{3}{4}$ (38) of the States — $\frac{3}{4}$

The Framers provided two ways for proposing amendments and two ways for ratifying them.

The First Amendment guarantees of freedom of assembly and petition enabled these supporters of the Equal Rights Amendment to demonstrate in front of the White House.

- The 13th Amendment ended slavery and forbade other forms of forced labor, except in prisons.
- The 14th Amendment defined citizenship; its due process and equal protection clauses protect civil rights from infringement by the states.
- The 15th Amendment prohibits any restrictions on the right to vote that are based on race, color, or having been a slave.

Later Amendments. Amendments 16 through 27 cover a variety of issues from an income tax to congressional pay raises.

- The 16th Amendment authorizes a federal income tax.
- The 17th Amendment establishes the direct election of U.S. senators.
- The 18th Amendment prohibits the sale and consumption of alcohol, and is the only amendment that was **repealed**.
- The 19th Amendment gives women the right to vote.
- The 20th Amendment changed the starting dates for presidential and congressional terms.
- The 21st Amendment repealed Prohibition (Amendment 18), the only amendment ever ratified by state conventions.

Six amendments have been ratified since 1950.

- The 22nd Amendment limits the President to two terms of office.
- The 23rd Amendment gives citizens in the District of Columbia the right to vote for President and Vice President.
- The 24th Amendment prohibits the payment of a tax as a qualification for voting in federal elections.
- The 25th Amendment set forth the procedures for determining presidential disability, presidential succession, and filling a vice presidential vacancy.
- The 26th Amendment establishes the minimum age for voting at 18.
- The 27th Amendment states that congressional pay raises take effect after the next congressional election.

repeal *to remove or cancel a law*

Name _____ Date _____

2 Review

1. Defining Constitutional Terms
Write a brief definition for each of the following terms.

a. amend _____

b. joint resolution _____

c. due process _____

d. civil _____

e. bail _____

f. repeal _____

2. Reviewing Social Studies Skills: Reading a Chart
On the chart below, circle the amendments that expanded voting rights.

Amendment	Subject	Year Adopted
1–10	Bill of Rights	1791
11	Immunity of states from certain suits	1795
12	Changes in electoral college procedure	1804
13	Prohibition of slavery	1865
14	Citizenship, due process, and equal protection of the law	1868
15	Prohibits denial of the vote because of race, color, or previous condition of slavery	1870
16	Power of Congress to tax incomes	1913
17	Direct election of senators	1913
18	Prohibition on the sale and consumption of liquor	1919
19	Right to vote for women	1920
20	Change of dates for presidential and congressional terms	1933
21	Repeal of Amendment 18	1933
22	Limit on presidential terms	1951
23	Electoral vote for the District of Columbia	1961
24	Prohibition of tax payment as a qualification to vote in federal elections	1964
25	Presidential disability and succession	1967
26	Minimum age for voting set at 18	1971
27	Congressional pay	1992

3. Reviewing the Main Ideas
Using complete sentences, write a brief answer for each of the following questions.

a. In what two ways can the Constitution be amended? _____

b. What fundamental rights are protected by the First Amendment? _____

c. How was the amendment process used to improve the lives of former slaves after the Civil War?

_____

4. Critical Thinking Skills: Understanding the Constitution
On a separate sheet of paper, write a paragraph to answer the following question.

If you had an opportunity to add an amendment to the Constitution, what would you propose? Why?

Informal Changes

As you read, think about the answers to these questions:

➤ How has the way the Framers wrote the Constitution affected constitutional change?

➤ How have the actions of Congress and Presidents changed the Constitution?

➤ What role has custom played in changing the Constitution?

➤ What effect have court decisions had on the Constitution?

Through the process of formal amendment, Congress and the states have eliminated some words from the original Constitution and added new ones. Many other changes have occurred informally and have not altered the Constitution's actual words. These informal changes have influenced how the government operates, and they continue to shape American society.

Use of Broad Language

In a sense, the Framers provided only the skeleton for a government—a framework that future Presidents, Congresses, and Supreme Courts had to flesh out. They set forth general principles and used broad language. As those words are reread, reinterpreted, and reapplied, informal changes in the meaning of the Constitution occur.

For example, the Constitution's opening words are "We the People of the United States . . ." In 1787 *people* referred to white males who owned property. Today that word includes all men and women, of all races, no matter how much money or property they have. As the attitudes and beliefs of the American people have changed, so too has the meaning of the Constitution. Such informal changes are also made by actions of Congress, the President, and the courts, as well as by several common political practices that have developed over the last 200 years.

Filling in the Details

Congress and the executive branch have both played important roles in changing the Constitution. Some of these changes occurred in the first decade after the Constitution took effect. Others evolved slowly over the next two centuries.

Congress. The Framers intended that Congress fill in the details that were missing from many sections of the Constitution. For instance, the elastic clause (Article 1, Section 8, Clause 18) states that Congress has the authority to make any laws "which shall be necessary and proper" for carrying out its specific powers. This clause gives Congress a great deal of freedom to define and extend its powers.

Similarly, the Constitution's commerce clause (Article 1, Section 8, Clause 3) grants Congress the power to regulate foreign and interstate commerce. But the Constitution does not say exactly what *regulate* means, nor does it define *commerce*. As a result, Congress has used this clause widely, for example, to build hydroelectric dams, prohibit racial discrimination on buses, and construct the interstate highway system.

Chief Executives. Presidents also have had an informal but significant impact on the Constitution when they have acted to expand their powers. President Thomas Jefferson did so when he agreed to purchase the Louisiana Territory from France in 1803. He faced a dilemma because the Constitution did not say whether the government could buy land from a foreign country. Jefferson had long argued that the government had only those powers spelled out in the Constitution, but he realized how valuable the land would be to the new nation. He decided that the President's power to make treaties with foreign nations gave him the authority to make the Louisiana Purchase. After a long and bitter debate, Congress agreed with him and ratified the treaty with France in October 1803. The effect of Jefferson's decision was to expand the powers of the presidency by interpreting the Constitution broadly. The words of the Constitution remained the same, but their meaning had changed.

In some cases, Presidents have expanded their powers so much that Congress has tried to rein them in. For example, the Constitution says that the President is commander in chief of the armed forces but that only Congress may declare war. On more than 150 occasions, however, Presidents have sent troops into combat abroad without congressional declarations of war. Although Congress never declared war on Vietnam, half a million American troops fought in that conflict. Congress became so concerned about the President's power that in 1973 it passed the War Powers Act. This legislation placed restrictions on the President's ability to use troops in combat without congressional approval.

Presidents have also found a way to make treaties with foreign nations without obtaining approval from the Senate, as required by the Constitution. Presidents have made pacts called executive agreements with the heads of other countries. Because these agreements are not formal treaties, Presidents can use them to conduct foreign policy without asking the Senate.

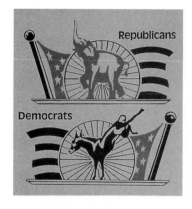

Over the years, the elephant and the donkey have been accepted as symbols of the Republican and Democratic parties, respectively.

Customs Shape the Constitution's Meaning

Certain other customs have developed in our system of government over the years. These common practices are, for the most part, unwritten. Yet government officials follow them with care and consistency.

political party *organized group of people that seeks to control government through the winning of elections and the holding of public office*

nomination *process of selecting candidates to run for public office*

Cabinet *advisory board composed of the heads of the executive departments*

succession *process of taking over a title or office from the person who held it before*

Political Parties. America's two-party political system is a good example of such customs. A **political party** is a group of people who share political beliefs and seek to control the government by winning elections. For much of our country's history, two major parties have dominated American politics. The Constitution does not mention political parties. But since the late 1790s, they have played a major role in shaping the government.

The Constitution is also silent about the nomination of candidates for the presidency. Since the 1830s, however, political parties have been holding special nominating conventions. State legislatures have also altered the electoral college procedures by usually requiring that delegates follow the popular vote of each state in presidential elections.

Other Customs. Beginning with George Washington, Presidents have called on the heads of their executive departments—the Cabinet—for advice. Today it is difficult to imagine our government without the Cabinet. It has assumed an accepted and essential place in the executive branch of the government.

Custom has also determined what happens when a President dies. The original Constitution did not actually spell out the process of succession. It said that the powers and duties of the presidency—but not the office itself—should be transferred to the Vice President. But by custom, eight Vice Presidents succeeded to the office of the President who died. The passage of the 25th Amendment in 1967 formalized the practice.

Court Decisions Redefine the Constitution. Perhaps no department or branch of government has had as great an influence on the Constitution as the courts. Through the process of judicial review, the federal courts and the Supreme Court decide what the broad language of the Constitution actually means. The courts can rule that acts of Congress and the President are unconstitutional and, therefore, invalid.

The process of informal constitutional change has played a key role in the development of the American system of government. Many historians feel that it has had an even greater impact on the Constitution than the formal amendment process. Although the Framers could not foresee how their descendants would alter the Constitution, they intended all along that it be a living document—one that could evolve to meet society's changing needs.

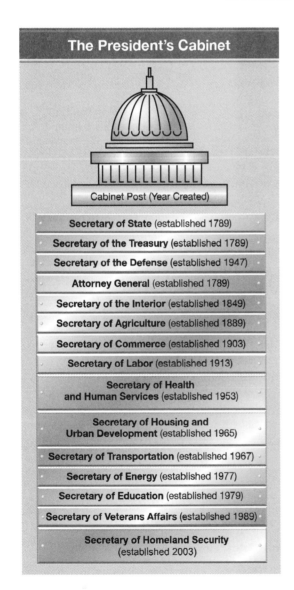

The President's Cabinet

Cabinet Post (Year Created)

Secretary of State (established 1789)

Secretary of the Treasury (established 1789)

Secretary of the Defense (established 1947)

Attorney General (established 1789)

Secretary of the Interior (established 1849)

Secretary of Agriculture (established 1889)

Secretary of Commerce (established 1903)

Secretary of Labor (established 1913)

Secretary of Health and Human Services (established 1953)

Secretary of Housing and Urban Development (established 1965)

Secretary of Transportation (established 1967)

Secretary of Energy (established 1977)

Secretary of Education (established 1979)

Secretary of Veterans Affairs (established 1989)

Secretary of Homeland Security (established 2003)

George Washington's Cabinet consisted of the heads of five executive departments: State, Treasury, War, Attorney General, and Postmaster General.

SECTION

3 Review

1. Defining Constitutional Terms

Write a brief definition for each of the following terms.

a. political party _____

b. nomination _____

c. succession _____

d. Cabinet _____

2. Reviewing Social Studies Skills: Distinguishing Fact from Opinion

Read the statements below and decide whether each one is a fact or an opinion. Then write "fact" or "opinion" in the spaces provided.

a. The process of formal amendment is much more important
than the process of informal amendment. _____

b. Jefferson violated the Constitution when he decided to buy
the Louisiana Territory. _____

c. The elastic clause gives Congress the freedom to define and
extend its powers. _____

d. America's two-party system is almost certainly unconstitutional. _____

e. The process of informal constitutional change has had a greater
effect on the Constitution than the formal process of amending it. _____

3. Reviewing the Main Ideas

Using complete sentences, write a brief answer for each of the following questions.

a. How do the broad language and general principles of the Constitution affect constitutional change?

_____

_____

b. What are some of the ways in which Congress and the President have made informal constitutional changes?

_____

_____

c. How have customs shaped the practices of the government? _____

_____

d. What important power does judicial review give to the Supreme Court? _____

_____

4. Critical Thinking Skills: Understanding the Constitution

On a separate sheet of paper, write a paragraph to answer the following question.

If the Framers had filled the Constitution with details and specific guidelines, how would it have affected the process of informal change?

You Are the Judge

Goss v. Lopez

Setting the Scene

You're in the school cafeteria eating lunch when you hear a noise across the room. You look up and see some students fighting and yelling. You can't quite hear what it's about, but you see it's becoming violent. The next thing you know, plates are flying, students are on the floor, and people are injured. Something flies by. Within minutes, you're on the floor, your pant leg is torn, you've got food in your hair, and the police are taking control.

The principal decides to suspend everyone who looks like they were involved in the melee, including you. But you hadn't done anything. Is this fair? More important, is it legal?

The Issue: Due Process

Are students protected by the right to due process? (Recall that the 5th Amendment protects due process at the federal level while the 14th protects it at the State and local level.) In October 1974 the U.S. Supreme Court heard arguments in a case that decided just this question. The case, *Goss v. Lopez,* involved students from several public high schools in Columbus, Ohio. All of the students had been suspended from school without a hearing.

Students Speak up for Their Rights

Political protests were common in the 1970s, even in high schools. In February and March 1971, violent political demonstrations broke out at two Columbus high schools. In one school, students created a disturbance in a lunchroom that eventually involved dozens of students and damaged school property. In the other, a student demonstration in an auditorium led to school officials calling in the police.

In both incidents, students were arrested and taken to the police station. All students suspected of being involved in these demonstrations were immediately suspended from school for ten days.

The School Requires Discipline

Many students protested. They said the suspensions were unfair. Some claimed they were not involved in the demonstrations. They wanted to know exactly what they were accused of, and they wanted a chance to explain their side of the story.

No opportunity was given, however. School officials said they had to move quickly to discipline the students. School board policy was that school administrators could suspend students from school without offering them any sort of hearing or the chance to tell their side of the story. Suspension is a form of discipline and in the schools, the principal has the authority to administer it.

Students protested that suspension leaves a serious and damaging mark on their records and that they should have a chance to speak on something this important. The school replied that getting poor grades is important, as is making the football team, yet no one is entitled to a hearing after failing a test or being cut from the football team. There's nothing different here, they said.

The Students Respond

The students believed that they were entitled to their 14th Amendment right of due process and the right to a hearing before being punished. Students representing three high schools filed a class action lawsuit—a lawsuit brought by a small number of people on behalf of a much larger number who face the same issue—against the school board. They claimed they were suspended without due process.

The first court to hear the case was the U.S. District Court in Columbus. This three-judge panel ruled in favor of the students. The court said that students facing suspension were entitled to written notice and a hearing. If necessary—for example, if the student's conduct is disruptive or dangerous to the school—the suspension can begin before the hearing. In any case, however, the school must notify the parents within 24 hours, in writing, that there will be a suspension hearing. The school must hold a suspension hearing, with the student present, within 72 hours of the student's removal from school. At the hearing, the student and others must be permitted to make statements in the student's defense.

The Columbus School District then appealed the case to the U.S. Supreme Court. On October 16, 1974, the Supreme Court heard arguments from both sides in the dispute.

Arguments for the School District

1. Because there is no constitutional right to an education at public expense, the due process clause of the 14th Amendment does not protect against suspensions from the public school system.

2. The district must have broad authority over student behavior and must be able to act quickly to bring order. It's too great a burden to ask that the district hold hearings every time a student is suspended.

Arguments for the Students

1. If the state chooses to give students a free education, that becomes a right that the state cannot withdraw without due process.

2. Suspending a student from school can damage his or her reputation and prospects for their future success. Doing so without giving the person an opportunity to explain what happened is a violation of the person's liberty.

Conclusion

In January 1975 the Supreme Court issued a ruling in this case. What are the constitutional and legal issues raised by this case? Suppose you were writing the Court's opinion. In whose favor would you decide—for the students or for the school district? If the students are entitled to due process, do you think the protections offered by the District Court are sufficient? Do you think they give too much protection?

4

The Supreme Court and the Constitution

DECISIONS, DECISIONS, DECISIONS

A political cartoonist summarizes the work of the Supreme Court.

About This Chapter

Every year the Supreme Court is asked to review thousands of cases. Of these, the justices hear about a hundred. In deciding which cases to review, the Court considers the importance of the underlying issues to American society at the time. As the attitudes of Americans change, the opinions of the Court may also change. Issues that were decided years ago may come before the Court again, and the justices may issue a different ruling. Similarly, the Court might decide to hear a case that a previous Supreme Court refused to hear.

The Supreme Court plays a crucial role in American society. The Court's rulings have affected how the government works and how Americans live their lives. Some cases are so controversial that many Americans await the Court's rulings with excitement or dread, depending on their points of view.

Judicial Review

As you read, think about the answers to these questions:

➤ How did the powers of the Supreme Court evolve?

➤ Why was the case of *Marbury* v. *Madison* so important?

➤ What events during and after the Civil War expanded the Supreme Court's power?

The primary responsibility of the Supreme Court is to judge whether the laws and actions of Congress and the President are administered fairly. This function is known as judicial review, but that term appears nowhere in the Constitution. This important power was developed through interpretation, **landmark** decisions, and a constitutional amendment.

landmark *event or development that marks a turning point*

Powers Defined Through Interpretation

Article III of the Constitution calls for the establishment of a Supreme Court and other lower federal courts. But like many aspects of the

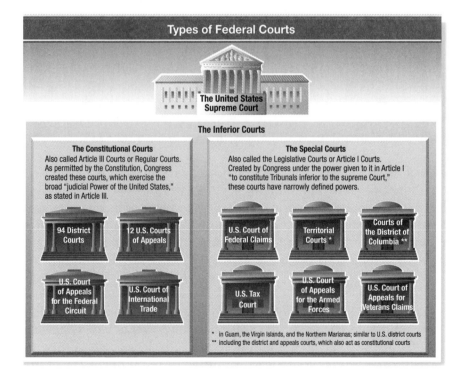

Types of Federal Courts

The United States Supreme Court

The Inferior Courts

The Constitutional Courts
Also called Article III Courts or Regular Courts. As permitted by the Constitution, Congress created these courts, which exercise the broad "judicial Power of the United States," as stated in Article III.

94 District Courts

12 U.S. Courts of Appeals

U.S. Court of Appeals for the Federal Circuit

U.S. Court of International Trade

The Special Courts
Also called the Legislative Courts or Article I Courts. Created by Congress under the power given to it in Article I "to constitute Tribunals inferior to the supreme Court," these courts have narrowly defined powers.

U.S. Court of Federal Claims

Territorial Courts *

Courts of the District of Columbia **

U.S. Tax Court

U.S. Court of Appeals for the Armed Forces

U.S. Court of Appeals for Veterans Claims

* in Guam, the Virgin Islands, and the Northern Marianas; similar to U.S. district courts
** including the district and appeals courts, which also act as constitutional courts

Article III of the Constitution established the Supreme Court and gave Congress the power to create the lower federal courts.

Constitution, the meaning of Article III—and its implementation—was left open to interpretation by Congress.

The first Congress passed the Judiciary Act of 1789, establishing the Supreme Court, 3 circuit courts, and 15 district courts. Congress also appointed a Chief Justice and five associate justices to serve on the Supreme Court. Yet the Court's powers were still largely undefined. Through the Court's interpretation of the Constitution in particular cases, its powers were gradually defined. The first three Chief Justices had little impact on the direction of the Court. But the actions of the fourth are still felt today.

Landmark Case Defines Judicial Review

On February 17, 1801, President John Adams, a member of the Federalist Party, lost his bid for reelection to Thomas Jefferson, a Democratic-Republican. Even before the presidential election was decided by the House of Representatives, it was clear that the Federalists also lost control of Congress. For the few months before the new President and Congress took office, Adams and his party still had control. Adams used that time to take actions that would bolster the Federalist position in government.

Adams Packs the Courts. President Adams persuaded Congress to pass the Judiciary Act of 1801, which gave him the power to appoint new federal judges. Adams appointed 39 new judges who shared his political beliefs and who would likely oppose Jefferson's policies. But at the end of his term, Adams's secretary of state had failed to deliver three of the commissions for the new posts. One of the commissions was for William Marbury.

Madison Denies Marbury's Commission. When Jefferson became President in March 1801, he discovered the undelivered commissions and instructed his secretary of state, James Madison, to refuse the appointments. William Marbury, angry and frustrated, took his case to the Supreme Court in an attempt to gain his post. He asked the Court for a writ of mandamus, forcing Madison to make him a judge.

Marshall's Ruling. Chief Justice John Marshall sympathized with Marbury but ruled that the Judiciary Act of 1789, by which Congress gave the Supreme Court the power to issue a writ of mandamus, was unconstitutional. In Marshall's opinion, Congress could not give the Court this power; only the Constitution could, and that document said nothing about it.

William Marbury never became a federal judge. But the Court's ruling in *Marbury* v. *Madison* established a very important precedent, which has served as a guide for later cases. Marshall interpreted the Constitution to mean that the Court had the power of judicial review and could overturn laws that it determined to be unconstitutional. Marshall pointed out that the Constitution is the "supreme law of the

John Marshall served as the fourth Chief Justice of the Supreme Court. Many landmark cases were decided during his term on the High Court.

commission *legal document that authorizes a person to perform certain official duties*

writ of mandamus *document that orders a public official to perform certain duties*

precedent *legal decision that serves as a guide for similar cases in the future*

land" and that the Supreme Court has the final say over what is, and is not, in accordance with the Constitution.

Court's Power Expanded After the Civil War

The influence of the Supreme Court was further expanded after the American Civil War. Two important occurrences contributed to the Court's increased authority.

Ex Parte Milligan.
In 1866 the Supreme Court made a ruling in the case *Ex parte Milligan,* which means "on behalf of Milligan." Milligan was a northerner who supported the Confederate cause and was accused of encouraging rebellion in Indiana. President Abraham Lincoln issued a military order for his arrest. Milligan's lawyers, however, argued that Lincoln had violated a constitutional protection against unjust arrest and imprisonment.

The Constitution says that during wartime, the federal government can impose military rule and suspend courts' ability to issue writs of habeas corpus. Lincoln had done just that in 1861, when the Civil War erupted. But the Supreme Court ruled that neither the President nor Congress has the right to suspend habeas corpus throughout the United States, unless the whole country is the scene of actual fighting. Milligan's conviction was overturned because there was no fighting in Indiana when he was arrested.

writ of habeas corpus *court order requiring the government to release a prisoner unless good cause for imprisonment can be shown*

The Court also drew limits on the government's ability to impose military rule. This case further demonstrated that the Supreme Court had the power to judge whether the acts of the executive and legislative branches were constitutional.

The Fourteenth Amendment.
In 1868 the states ratified the 14th Amendment, which requires states to obey federal laws. This amendment increased the jurisdiction, or authority, of the Supreme Court. The 14th Amendment had little impact until the 1920's, however, when the Court began to use it to rule on the constitutionality of state laws as well as federal laws.

jurisdiction *area of authority*

SECTION

1 Review

1. Defining Constitutional Terms

Write a brief definition for each of the following terms.

a. landmark _____

b. commission _____

c. writ of mandamus _____

d. precedent _____

e. writ of habeas corpus _____

f. jurisdiction _____

2. Reviewing Social Studies Skills: Sequencing Events

The five items below defined and expanded the Supreme Court's power of judicial review. Place them in the order in which they occurred by writing the numbers 1 through 5 in the space provided.

Ex parte Milligan   _____

14th Amendment   _____

Judiciary Act of 1789   _____

Marbury v. *Madison*   _____

Judiciary Act of 1801   _____

3. Reviewing the Main Ideas

Using complete sentences, write a brief answer for each of the following questions.

a. What does the Constitution say about the Supreme Court's power of judicial review? _____

_____

_____

_____

b. What arguments did John Marshall use to support his opinion in the case of *Marbury* v. *Madison?*

_____

_____

_____

c. How did the 14th Amendment increase the power of the Supreme Court? _____

_____

_____

_____

4. Critical Thinking Skills: Understanding the Constitution

On a separate sheet of paper, write a brief paragraph to answer the following question.

If the Supreme Court did not have the power of judicial review, how would the balance of power among the three branches of government be affected?

2 First Amendment Freedoms

As you read, think about the answers to these questions:

➤ How does the First Amendment protect freedom of religion?

➤ What has the Court said about freedom of speech?

➤ How have Supreme Court decisions affected freedom of the press?

The First Amendment to the Constitution states that "Congress shall make no law respecting an establishment of religion, or prohibiting the free exercise thereof; or abridging the freedom of speech, or of the press; or of the people peaceably to assemble, and to petition the government for a redress of grievances." Like much of the Constitution, the First Amendment says much in few words. But those words created a complex debate that still goes on—how to balance the rights of the individual with the needs of society.

Many Americans believe that the First Amendment gives them the right to think, say, or write whatever they choose. Others believe that an individual's actions should never endanger the rights of the majority of citizens. The Supreme Court has had the challenge of interpreting the First Amendment through cases that come before it. The cases described below are a few examples of the specific and complicated situations that the Court considered. Sometimes the Court has upheld First Amendment rights, but at other times it has placed limits on those freedoms. The cases described below are examples of some of the First Amendment cases that the Supreme Court has considered.

Clauses to Protect Freedom of Religion

The First Amendment reflects the belief of the Framers that religious and political matters should be separate. In practice, however, the separation of church and state is not always obvious. For example, the government supports religion by allowing religious groups not to pay property taxes, and both the currency of the United States and the Pledge of Allegiance make reference to God. The First Amendment protects religious freedom in two clauses: the establishment clause and the free exercise clause.

The Establishment Clause. The establishment clause states that "Congress shall make no law respecting an establishment of religion . . . ," thus prohibiting the government from establishing a national religion.

establishment clause *part of the First Amendment that prohibits the government from setting up a national religion*

nonsectarian *not associated with a particular religious group*

free exercise clause *part of the First Amendment that prohibits the government from interfering in Americans' free exercise of their religious beliefs*

polygamy *marriage in which a spouse may have more than one mate at the same time*

Angered that the National Rifle Association held its annual convention in Denver after the high school shooting in nearby Littleton, protesters exercise their First Amendment right to protest.

Most of the Court's rulings on this clause have been issued during the last 60 years.

- *Everson* v. *Board of Education* (1947) involved a New Jersey law that provided public government funding to transport children to private religious schools. Opponents of the law argued that it violated the establishment clause, but the Supreme Court disagreed. The Court ruled that aid to children did not constitute governmental support of religion.

- *Engel* v. *Vitale* (1962) was one of the most controversial Supreme Court decisions concerning the issue of prayer in public schools. The New York State Board of Regents had written a nonsectarian prayer and allowed students to recite it on a voluntary basis. The Court ruled that the government should not be writing prayers, nor should religious exercises be conducted in public schools.

The Free Exercise Clause.

The free exercise clause states that "Congress shall make no law . . . prohibiting the free exercise [of religion] . . ." This clause prohibits government from interfering in Americans' free exercise of their religious beliefs. The earliest Supreme Court decisions about church-state relations involved the Court's interpretation of the free exercise clause.

- *Reynolds* v. *United States* (1879) involved the prosecution of George Reynolds, a Mormon who had two wives. Although federal law prohibited polygamy, Reynolds's religion permitted the practice. The Supreme Court ruled that while he was free to believe what he wanted, his actions had to conform to federal laws. The Court's message was clear: The government could not regulate a person's beliefs, but it could regulate his or her actions.

- *Wisconsin* v. *Yoder* (1972) involved an Amish community that objected to sending their children to public schools after eighth grade, claiming that such exposure of their children to another culture would endanger the group's lifestyle, which was essential to their faith. The Court decided that requiring attendance of the Amish children in public school past the eighth grade would conflict with their ability to practice their religion, and would, therefore, be unconstitutional.

Freedom of Speech and Its Limitations

A democratic system of government works effectively only if citizens can openly express different points of view. Some of those opinions are likely to be unpopular. By guaranteeing freedom of speech, the First Amendment makes it possible for people to deal with the complicated issues of the day and make informed choices.

Like freedom of religion, however, freedom of speech is not absolute in the United States. The Supreme Court has placed restrictions on speech that seems to threaten the rights of others or the social order.

- *Schenck* v. *United States* (1919) involved Charles Schenck, an officer in an antiwar political group. He was arrested for alleged violations of the Espionage Act of 1917, which made active opposition to World War I a crime. Schenck had urged thousands of young men to resist the draft. The Court upheld limiting free speech in time of war, stating that Schenck's words presented a "clear and present danger" to society.

- *Gitlow* v. *New York* (1925) concerned the case of Benjamin Gitlow, who was convicted of publishing a pamphlet that called for the overthrow of all government and the establishment of socialism. Under New York law, such an act was illegal because it could possibly lead to social chaos. Gitlow's defense argued that the pamphlet was only a philosophical statement and did not create a "clear and present danger" of disrupting society. But the Court upheld the New York law and Gitlow's conviction, ruling that speech that had even a tendency to lead to harm could be found to be illegal.

Free Press Issues

Closely related to the issue of free speech is that of free press. As with other areas of the First Amendment, the Court has had to balance individual rights with those of society.

- *New York Times Co.* v. *Sullivan* (1964) set constitutional limits on **libel** law and expanded the protections for the press to criticize public officials. In this case, L. B. Sullivan claimed that an advertisement in the *New York Times* contained passages that falsely libeled him. The ad contained several inaccuracies, and Sullivan brought suit against the newspaper for not checking the facts before publishing the ad. The Court ruled that Sullivan could not collect damages unless it could be proved that the libelous statements had been made with "actual malice"—with the knowledge that the statements were false, or with reckless disregard of whether they were false.

- *New York Times Co.* v. *United States* (1971) pitted freedom of the press against national security. During the Vietnam War, the U.S. government obtained a temporary restraining order to prevent the *New York Times* and the *Washington Post* from publishing classified documents. The documents revealed that the United States was more heavily involved in the Vietnamese civil war than public officials had admitted. The government claimed that the publication of the so-called Pentagon Papers would harm the security of the nation. By a vote of 6–3, the Court ruled in favor of the newspapers, finding that the government had failed to meet "the heavy burden of showing justification" for prohibiting the newspapers from publishing the Pentagon Papers.

The cases described here represent only a fraction of the total number of First Amendment cases the Supreme Court has considered. They are, however, sufficient to show how the high court has confronted the issue of balancing the rights of the individual with the needs of society.

libel *intentional injury to a person's reputation*

SECTION

2 Review

1. Defining Constitutional Terms

Write a brief definition for each of the following terms.

a. establishment clause _____

_____

b. free exercise clause _____

_____

c. libel _____

_____

2. Reviewing Social Studies Skills: Classifying Facts

The cases described in this lesson concerned the freedoms of religion, speech, and the press. In the space provided next to each case, write the freedom with which the case is associated.

Wisconsin v. *Yoder*   _____

Schenck v. *United States*   _____

New York Times Co. v. *Sullivan*   _____

Gitlow v. *New York*   _____

Engel v. *Vitale*   _____

3. Reviewing the Main Ideas

Using complete sentences, write a brief answer for each of the following questions.

a. In what two ways does the First Amendment protect freedom of religion? _____

_____

_____

_____

b. What kinds of speech has the Court refused to protect under the First Amendment? _____

_____

_____

_____

c. How did the Supreme Court decision in *New York Times Co.* v. *Sullivan* affect freedom of the press?

_____

_____

_____

4. Critical Thinking Skills: Understanding the Constitution

On a separate sheet of paper, write a paragraph to answer the following question.

Do you agree or disagree that the Supreme Court's decision in *Engel* v. *Vitale* limits freedom of religion? Explain your answer.

Rights of the Accused

As you read, think about the answers to these questions:

➤ Which amendments protect the rights of the accused?

➤ Why is it important that people accused of committing crimes be presumed innocent?

➤ What are the two kinds of due process?

➤ How has the Supreme Court redefined the rights of the accused?

Three of the amendments in the Bill of Rights are intended to protect people accused of crimes from unfair treatment by the government. In applying these amendments, the Supreme Court has had to maintain a delicate balance between the accused person's right to be treated fairly and the majority's right to be protected from criminals.

Protecting the Rights of the Accused

The Fifth, Sixth, and Eighth Amendments were written to protect the rights of individuals accused of breaking society's laws. They seek to guarantee that the government does not abuse its power to administer justice. These amendments are based on an English tradition referred to as presumption of innocence, the idea that a person is presumed to be innocent unless and until he or she is proven guilty.

Reasoning Behind the Presumption. When an individual is accused of a crime, the accused and the accuser are not equal. The government (accuser) has police officers, prosecutors, and other members of the criminal justice system on its side. Against these powerful forces stands the accused individual.

When a person is presumed innocent, the government must assume the burden of proof. That is, the government must convince a jury that the accused person actually committed the crime. The individual is not required to prove innocence, only to show that the government's evidence is faulty or insufficient. In order to convict, the jury must be convinced that not even a "reasonable doubt" remains about the accused person's guilt.

Problems With the Presumption. Presumption of innocence means that sometimes the government is unable to punish a person who really did break a law. If the government knows that it lacks convincing

presumption of innocence *assumption that someone is innocent until proven guilty of a crime*

prosecutor *government official who seeks to prove the guilt of an accused person*

PRIMARY SOURCES

"It is better to risk saving a guilty person than to condemn an innocent one."
—*Voltaire*

evidence against an accused person, it may simply release the person. The government may also **plea bargain** in order to obtain a conviction on a less serious charge.

Expanding Due Process

The Fifth Amendment guarantees "due process of law" to the accused. Originally this requirement applied only to rules that the national government had to follow. In the 20th century, the Supreme Court has used the 14th Amendment to rule that states must also follow the rules of due process.

plea bargain process by which an accused person agrees to plead guilty to a less serious crime

Procedural and Substantive Due Process. There are two kinds of due process:

- Procedural due process means that the government follows the rules by which it has agreed to treat accused individuals.

- Substantive due process means that the laws themselves are fair and constitutional.

Due Process Procedures. Procedural due process protects the rights of persons accused of crimes from the time they are arrested through the time they are found guilty or not guilty. Due process includes the following:

probable cause valid reason for a police search or arrest

- The arrest must be based on **probable cause** (such as a police officer witnessing a crime) or on a warrant issued by a judge.

- The arrested person must be informed of his or her right to remain silent and to have the assistance of a lawyer. The accused individual cannot be forced to confess.

grand jury group of people selected to hear evidence and decide whether a person should be charged with a crime

- A **grand jury** or prosecutor must determine that enough evidence exists to bring the alleged criminal to trial.

- The accused person is entitled to be informed of the charge and to receive a speedy and public trial by jury.

- During the trial, the prosecution must prove to an unbiased jury that the defendant is guilty, beyond a reasonable doubt.

- The defendant can refuse to answer questions that would imply his or her own guilt.

- The defendant has the right to question his or her accusers and to demand the testimony of witnesses in his or her favor.

- If the jury finds the defendant not guilty, the accused individual cannot be tried again on the same charge.

- If the jury finds the person guilty, he or she may appeal the verdict to a higher court for review.

Redefining the Rights of the Accused

The amendments dealing with the rights of the accused have been redefined by the Supreme Court. In several very important cases, the Court has decided that accused individuals should have the same constitutional protections in state courts that they have in federal courts.

Mapp v. _Ohio._ In this famous 1961 decision, the Court declared that evidence that the police obtained illegally could not be used in a state court against the person from whom it was taken. In this case, the police had entered a woman's home—without a warrant and without her permission—looking for gambling materials. Instead, the police found obscene books, for which the woman was arrested and convicted. The Supreme Court said that the police had violated the Fourth Amendment's protection against illegal searches and seizures. Therefore, the books found during the search could not be used against the woman.

Gideon v. _Wainwright._ Similarly, a 1963 decision extended the Sixth Amendment's guarantee of an attorney to poor people who had committed relatively minor crimes. This case concerned a Florida man, Clarence Earl Gideon, who was too poor to hire a lawyer. The judge denied his request for a lawyer. Forced to represent himself, Gideon was convicted of breaking into a poolroom and was sentenced to five years in prison.

From his prison cell, Gideon asked the Supreme Court to review his case. The Court agreed to hear him and, using the 14th Amendment as its guide, unanimously decided in Gideon's favor. As a result, every accused person now enjoys the right to a lawyer even if the government must pay the lawyer's fee.

Miranda v. _Arizona._ In 1966 the Supreme Court ruled that since the Fifth Amendment gives an accused person the right not to incriminate himself or herself, confessions obtained by the police are not valid if the accused person is not aware of this right. In the _Miranda_ case, the police had questioned a man named Ernesto Miranda without informing him of his rights, and Miranda confessed to kidnapping and rape. His confession was later used in court to help convict him. However, the Supreme Court reversed Miranda's conviction and established guidelines that police must follow before they can question suspects. According to the "Miranda Rule," suspects must be told

- That they have a right to refuse to answer questions;

- That what they tell the police can be used against them in court;

- That they have a right to an attorney even if they cannot afford to hire one; and

- That even if they have answered some questions, they may refuse to answer any more at any time.

Some Americans believe that the judicial balance has swung in favor of the lawbreakers and against the society's right to protection from criminals. As the history of the Court shows, the task of redefining the Constitution is a job that is never finished.

Because the American system of justice is based on the presumption of innocence, the Constitution provides measures to protect rights of the accused.

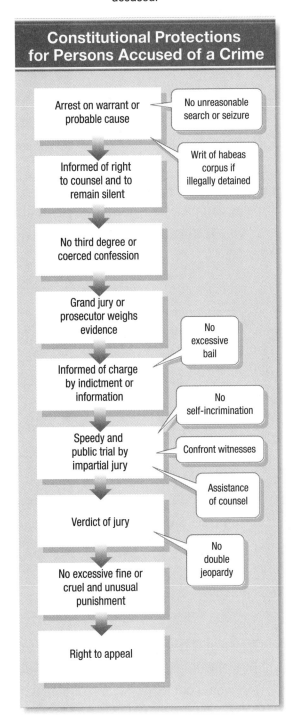

Constitutional Protections for Persons Accused of a Crime

SECTION

3 Review

1. Defining Constitutional Terms

Write a brief definition for each of the following terms.

a. presumption of innocence _____

b. prosecutor _____

c. plea bargain _____

d. probable cause _____

e. grand jury _____

2. Reviewing Social Studies Skills: Drawing Conclusions

Answer the following question in two or three sentences.

Based on its rulings in *Mapp* v. *Ohio* (1961), *Gideon* v. *Wainwright* (1963), and *Miranda* v. *Arizona* (1966), what conclusions can you draw about the character of the Supreme Court in the early and mid-1960s?

3. Reviewing the Main Ideas

Using complete sentences, write a brief answer for each of the following questions.

a. Which amendments in the Bill of Rights protect the rights of the accused? _____

_____

_____

_____

b. Why is the presumption of innocence such an important principle in our legal system? _____

_____

_____

_____

c. Explain the two types of due process. _____

_____

_____

_____

d. How have Supreme Court decisions affected the rights of the accused during the past four decades?

_____

_____

_____

4. Critical Thinking Skills: Understanding the Constitution

On a separate sheet of paper, write a paragraph to answer the following question.

How would our legal system be different if an accused person had to prove his or her innocence instead of the government having to prove that person's guilt?

Civil Rights

As you read, think about the answers to these questions:

➤ What role did the Supreme Court play in the struggle by African Americans to win their civil rights?

➤ How have other minority groups and women used the courts to defend their civil rights?

The original purpose of the Bill of Rights was to prevent the national government from abusing the liberty of individuals. The Constitution said nothing, however, about the states having to obey these amendments. In 1868 Congress passed the 14th Amendment, prohibiting the states from denying people their rights and due process. It calls for all people to have "equal protection of the laws."

The 14th Amendment was originally intended to establish and protect the rights of African American citizens after the Civil War. Over time, many other groups have turned to this amendment to protect their civil rights.

The Rights of African Americans

The passage of the 14th Amendment did not automatically end discrimination against black Americans. The Supreme Court had a narrow definition of discrimination, and it continued to let stand many racially biased laws. Not until 1954 did the Court finally overturn state laws that denied African Americans their basic liberties.

Dred Scott v. Sandford. The Court began hearing civil rights cases before the Civil War. One of the most famous cases involved Dred Scott, a black slave who lived with his master in the slave state of Missouri. For several years, however, they lived in the free state of Illinois

Martin Luther King, Jr.'s manner of nonviolent protest inspired the nation. Although decades have passed since he was assassinated, he remains one of the most respected civil rights leaders in history.

civil rights *basic freedoms guaranteed to citizens by the Constitution*

discrimination *policy or attitude that denies equal rights and treatment to certain groups of people*

segregate *to separate people on the basis of race, class, or ethnicity, or other differences*

Jim Crow laws *legislation passed by southern states in the 1800s and 1900s to force the segregation of the races; named for a character in minstrel shows of the 1800s that featured white actors in blackface makeup*

PRIMARY SOURCES

Our Constitution is color-blind, and neither knows nor tolerates classes among citizens. In respect of civil rights, all citizens are equal before the law. The humblest is the peer of the most powerful."
—Justice Harlan, dissenting opinion in Plessy v. Ferguson

and in the free territory of Minnesota. When he returned to Missouri, Scott sued for his freedom.

In 1857 the Supreme Court ruled that Scott was not an American citizen and, thus, had no right to sue in federal court. The Court said that Congress did not have the right to prevent citizens from carrying their slaves, or property, into free territories. This decision upheld the position of Southern slaveholders, and it pushed the already divided nation a step closer to civil war.

Plessy v. *Ferguson.*

In the 1880s and 1890s, many states moved to deprive black Americans of their civil rights and to segregate them from whites. Northern states segregated blacks through custom and private discrimination. Southern state legislatures, on the other hand, passed a series of Jim Crow laws. One of these laws, passed in Louisiana in 1890, required railroads to provide "separate but equal" accommodations for blacks and whites. When a black man named Homer Plessy refused to move from a seat in the white compartment of a railroad car, he was arrested and his case was eventually appealed to the Supreme Court.

In its 1896 decision the Supreme Court upheld the Louisiana law. The justices asserted that a law that recognizes differences in color "has no tendency to destroy the legal equality of the two races." The Court believed that the idea of "separate but equal" facilities was not a denial of equal protection under the law.

Brown v. *Board of Education of Topeka.*

Linda Carol Brown was an eight-year-old black girl who lived in Topeka, Kansas. State law required her to travel to a distant school for black students even though she lived just a few blocks from a school for white children. Linda's family sued the Topeka Board of Education.

In a historic 1954 decision, the Supreme Court completely reversed its ruling in *Plessy* v. *Ferguson.* Declaring that "separate educational facilities are inherently unequal," the Court added that the idea of separate but equal "has no place in public education." The Court ordered states to integrate their schools "with all deliberate speed."

This landmark decision heralded the beginning of the modern civil rights movement. Citing the 14th Amendment, civil rights leaders challenged discrimination in case after case during the next decade. Many people, both black and white, purposely broke segregation laws in order to challenge them in court. The Supreme Court supported them in dozens of these cases. The Court's decisions led to the passage of the Civil Rights Act of 1964 and the Voting Rights Act of 1965, in which Congress required that the federal government would uphold the rights of black Americans.

Civil Rights of Other Minorities

Blacks are not the only Americans who have suffered as a result of discrimination. Chinese Americans, Japanese Americans, Jews, Native Americans, Latinos, and women have all experienced prejudice and unequal treatment at various times in American history.

Korematsu* v. *United States. After the Japanese attack on Pearl Harbor in 1941, Japanese Americans became the target of hostility and discrimination. In 1942 defense officials labeled Japanese Americans a security risk, and the government forced tens of thousands of them into camps guarded by armed soldiers. Most had to sell their houses, businesses, and personal possessions at great losses. Fully two thirds of those evacuated were American-born citizens.

One of these people, Fred Korematsu, refused to obey the relocation order. After he was arrested, tried, and convicted, he appealed his case to the Supreme Court. He declared that he was an American citizen and loyal to his country. But the Court called the relocation program a "justifiable wartime measure" and decided that there was not enough time to identify which Japanese Americans were loyal and which were not.

Cleveland Board of Education* v. *LaFleur. The struggle of women for equal rights has also produced several important Supreme Court cases. In the early 1970s, Jo Carol LaFleur sued the Cleveland Board of Education. School board regulations required female teachers to take leave without pay at a certain point during pregnancy. The regulations also stated that these teachers could only return to work at the beginning of a new semester. LaFleur believed that these rules discriminated against women. In 1974 the Supreme Court agreed with LaFleur and declared that the regulations were unconstitutional under the 14th Amendment. The majority of the justices believed that the school board had no right to dictate a woman's personal choice in a family matter.

Many groups have turned to the Supreme Court to protect their equal rights. In recent decades it has tended to rule in their favor, expanding the definition of discrimination. This does not mean that discrimination has ceased to exist. Each year people continue to file suits claiming that their civil rights have been violated. Invariably these people look to the Bill of Rights and the 14th Amendment to defend their basic freedoms.

SECTION

4 Review

1. Defining Constitutional Terms
Write a brief definition for each of the following terms.

a. civil rights _____

b. discrimination _____

c. segregate _____

d. Jim Crow laws _____

2. Reviewing Social Studies Skills: Sequencing Events
Put the following Supreme Court decisions in chronological order by writing the numbers in the spaces provided at the right.

a. *Civil Rights Cases*   _____

b. *Brown* v. *Board of Education*   _____

c. *Cleveland Board of Education* v. *LaFleur*   _____

d. *Dred Scott* v. *Sandford*   _____

e. *Korematsu* v. *United States*   _____

f. *Plessy* v. *Ferguson*   _____

3. Reviewing the Main Ideas
Using complete sentences, write a brief answer for each of the following questions.

a. Which of the Supreme Court rulings discussed in this lesson helped black Americans gain their civil rights?

_____

_____

_____

b. Which of the Supreme Court rulings discussed in this lesson denied black Americans their civil rights?

_____

_____

_____

c. What other groups have turned to the Supreme Court to protect their civil rights? _____

_____

_____

_____

4. Critical Thinking Skills: Understanding the Constitution
On a separate sheet of paper, write a paragraph to answer the following question.

How has the 14th Amendment changed American society during the past 50 years?

As you read, think about the answers to these questions:

➤ Why has the Supreme Court held that laws calling for prayer in public schools are unconstitutional?

➤ Why did the Supreme Court rule that the death penalty is not cruel and unusual punishment?

➤ When are racial quotas considered a form of reverse discrimination?

➤ What limits has the Supreme Court placed on a woman's right to an abortion?

➤ What is the difference between judicial activism and judicial restraint?

Several crucial constitutional issues seem to remain unresolved. The Supreme Court continues to reexamine them in light of changing times and social attitudes. Among the most controversial of these recurring issues are school prayer, the death penalty, racial quotas, and abortion. Perhaps the most important issue is what role the Supreme Court should play in shaping social policy.

Rulings on School Prayer

When the Supreme Court banned the practice of voluntary school prayer in *Engel* v. *Vitale* (1962), the decision met with fierce opposition from some government officials and religious leaders. One senator believed that the high court had "made God unconstitutional." The justices, on the other hand, maintained that school prayer violated the First Amendment's establishment clause, which prohibits the government from establishing a state religion.

School District of Abington Township v. Schempp. In accordance with a state requirement, students at Abington Senior

The inscription over the main entrance to the Supreme Court building in Washington, D.C., reinforces the constitutional guarantee of due process for all.

High School in Pennsylvania began each day with a Bible reading broadcast over the school intercom. The Schempps, whose son attended the school, sued the school district for violating the establishment clause. They also argued that the school favored the Christian religion by supplying only a King James Bible for the readings. The district countered by saying that no religious instruction was involved and that participation was voluntary. In 1963 the Supreme Court ruled in the Schempps' favor, declaring that the state law was unconstitutional because it had a religious purpose.

***Wallace* v. *Jaffree*.** Twenty-two years later, the Court heard a challenge to an Alabama law that called for a one-minute period of silence in all public schools for meditation or voluntary prayer. Jaffree, a resident of Mobile, argued that the law lacked a secular purpose, and that its real purpose was to return prayer to the public schools, thereby violating the establishment clause.

secular *nonreligious; connected with everyday life*

In a 6–3 decision, the Supreme Court struck down the Alabama law. Since the *Wallace* decision, the Court has also ruled that the offering of prayer as part of a public school graduation ceremony is unconstitutional. That decision was handed down in a Rhode Island case known as *Lee* v. *Weisman* (1992).

Rulings on the Death Penalty

The issue of whether the death penalty violates the Eighth Amendment's ban on cruel and unusual punishment has come before the Supreme Court many times. Not until 1972, however, did the Court use the Eighth Amendment to strike down state death penalty laws.

Most of the cases come to the Supreme Court on appeal from lower courts. The Supreme Court does have original jurisdiction on cases involving a state or an ambassador.

***Furman* v. *Georgia*.** In a narrow 5–4 decision in this case, the Supreme Court effectively banned the death penalty in the United States in 1972.

Appealing a Case to the Supreme Court

Federal District Court

Federal Appeals Court

The United States Supreme Court

Step 1
Case is filed with or appealed to a federal district court.

Step 2
Case goes to a federal appeals court.

Step 3
Case is appealed to the Supreme Court. The Supreme Court either:

• allows the lower-court ruling to stand, or

• sends the case back to the lower court to reconsider it, or

• agrees to hear the case.

Step 4
Supreme Court rules on the case.

Of the five majority justices, two felt that the death penalty was cruel and unusual punishment in all circumstances; the other three objected to the way in which capital punishment was applied. Justices Douglas and Stewart found its application discriminatory, and Justice White found it "pointless and needless," since it was carried out so rarely. The four dissenting justices believed that repealing capital punishment was a matter for state legislatures to decide.

As a result of the *Furman* decision, 38 states passed new laws that limited juries' freedom in imposing the death penalty. By 1976 these new laws also came before the Court. Some of the new laws tried to satisfy the Court's objections by making the death penalty mandatory, or required, for first-degree murder. The Court has struck down some of them, ruling that mandatory death penalty laws violate the Eighth Amendment. The Court has allowed the death penalty for specific cases, such as for an accomplice to a murder only if that individual displayed "reckless indifference" to human life. The Court has also barred the execution of people for capital crimes committed before they were 16 or for those who are insane or unable to understand the reason for their execution.

capital punishment
penalty involving execution

Affirmative Action and Racial Quotas

The Civil Rights Act of 1964 banned discrimination from nearly all aspects of American life. The following year, the federal government began requiring schools and businesses to adopt affirmative action programs. These programs were aimed at ending the effects of past discrimination by giving favored treatment to minorities.

affirmative action *program aimed at ending the effects of past discrimination by giving favored treatment to minority groups*

Regents of University of California v. Bakke. By favoring minority group members over whites, however, affirmative action programs ran the risk of causing reverse discrimination. In the 1970s, Allan Bakke was refused admission to the medical school at the University of California at Davis. Of the 100 openings for new students, 16 were reserved for minority students. Bakke appeared to have better qualifications than some of the minority students who were accepted. As a result, he sued the university on the basis that the medical school's affirmative action program violated his 14th Amendment right to equal protection of the laws.

In 1978 the *Bakke* case resulted in two 5–4 Supreme Court rulings.

reverse discrimination *apparent bias that results from the attempt to undo past discrimination*

- In the first ruling, the majority said that the university's quota system was a violation of the Civil Rights Act of 1964. Reverse discrimination was illegal in any program receiving federal funds.

- In its second ruling, on the other hand, the Supreme Court approved affirmative action programs based on race as long as no rigid quotas were involved. Belonging to a minority group could be regarded as an asset for the student, something like an extracurricular activity or special talent, that a school might consider along with grades and other qualifications.

quota *number or amount constituting a proportional share*

In 1979 another quota case came before the high court. In *United Steel Workers* v. *Weber*, the Supreme Court ruled that, unlike public institutions that receive federal funds, private employers could use quotas in programs aimed at ending racial injustice.

The Right to Privacy

In one of the most controversial issues of the 20th century, the Court has had to decide if it is a crime for a woman to end her pregnancy. The right to choose an abortion, however, is part of a larger issue—the right of privacy.

Roe v. Wade. In the opinion he wrote for this historic 1973 case, Justice Harry A. Blackmun wrote that although the Constitution does not explicitly mention any right of privacy, the Court had recognized such a right in many of the cases it has heard. Blackmun was a member of the 7–2 majority that struck down a Texas law banning nearly all abortions.

The high court found that women had the right to end a pregnancy but that there are certain limits to this right. A state could still ban abortions during the final three months of pregnancy. In several cases since this landmark decision, the Court has expanded the possibility for state legislatures to adopt stricter limits to abortion. In two 1990 cases, for example, the Court ruled that a state may require a minor to tell one or both parents before having an abortion, except in cases where a judge gives her permission not to tell her parents.

Expanding the Court's Role

Through most of its history, the Supreme Court has not played an important role in making government policy. Using its power of judicial review cautiously, it has limited itself to striking down federal and state laws that are unconstitutional.

During the last half of the 20th century, however, the Court began taking a more active role in shaping public policy. In addressing the nation's social and political problems and ruling on constitutional questions whenever possible, the Court engages in judicial activism. The opposing approach, known as judicial restraint, holds that the Court should leave policy to the other branches of government and take action only when the Constitution has clearly been violated. Like other recurring issues, this debate has never been entirely resolved and probably will never completely disappear.

judicial activism *practice of basing decisions on what the Court perceives to ensure public welfare, or what the Court determines to be fair and just based on the facts it has been given*

judicial restraint *practice of basing decisions on previous decisions dealing with similar legal issues, and upholding a law if it does not clearly violate the Constitution*

Once referred to (by President Franklin Roosevelt) as "nine old men," the Supreme Court has changed in recent years to include women and minorities and to represent more diversity than ever before.

SECTION
5 Review

1. Defining Constitutional Terms
Write a brief definition for each of the following terms.

a. capital punishment _____

b. affirmative action _____

c. reverse discrimination _____

d. quota _____

e. judicial activism _____

f. judicial restraint _____

2. Reviewing Social Studies Skills: Recognizing Point of View
Circle the Supreme Court decisions that reflect judicial restraint.

School District of Abington Township v. *Schempp*

Furman v. *Georgia*

Regents of University of California v. *Bakke*

Roe v. *Wade*

3. Reviewing the Main Ideas
Using complete sentences, write a brief answer for each of the following questions.

a. On what grounds has the Supreme Court ruled against laws allowing prayer in public schools? _____
_____
_____

b. Why did the Supreme Court effectively ban the death penalty in the United States? _____
_____
_____

c. In the Court's view, when are racial quotas considered a form of reverse discrimination? _____
_____

d. In what ways has the Supreme Court limited a woman's right to an abortion? _____
_____

e. How is the philosophy of judicial activism different from the philosophy of judicial restraint? _____
_____
_____

4. Critical Thinking Skills: Understanding the Constitution
On a separate sheet of paper, write a paragraph to answer the following question.

What trend can you detect in the Supreme Court's decisions on school prayer cases beginning with *Engel* v. *Vitale?*

You Are the Judge

Santa Fe Independent School District v. Doe

Setting the Scene

The big high school football game is about to begin. As the band marches off the field, a student walks to the center yard line. "Let us bow our heads," he says. The crowd grows silent as he recites, "Dear Lord, thank you for allowing us to gather here tonight and please bless this game." Your best friend, who is sitting beside you, is Hindu. As the prayer continues, you see that she is becoming more and more uncomfortable.

The next day in school, she complains to the principal. He tells her that although prayer in the classroom is unconstitutional, it doesn't apply to a football game. Most of the students like the prayer, and if she's uncomfortable, she can simply skip the game. No one is forcing her to go.

If the prayer is making a student uncomfortable, is skipping the game her only choice? Is the school's action legal?

The Issue: First Amendment Rights

Is a public prayer before a high school football game a violation of the First Amendment prohibition against the establishment of religion by a government entity? In June 2000 the U.S. Supreme Court heard arguments in a case that decided just this question. The case, *Santa Fe Independent School District* v. *Doe,* involved students, their families, and the administration at Santa Fe High School in eastern Texas.

Establishment of Religion in Schools

The First Amendment to the U.S. Constitution says, "Congress shall make no law respecting an establishment of religion." This has generally been held to mean that no government body, such as a school district, can impose religious activities or religious beliefs on individuals. Many school activities have been challenged on this basis.

In 1962, in the case of *Engel* v. *Vitale,* the Supreme Court held that teachers could not lead students in prayer in the classroom. Thirty years later, in the case *Lee* v. *Weisman,* the Supreme Court said that public schools could not invite clergy members to school graduations to recite a prayer with the graduating class.

But what if, like the football game, it is not an official school event, but merely a school-sponsored event? And what if it is not a clergy member, but a fellow student, who leads the prayer? Does that make a difference?

A Long Tradition

Prayers before football games had been a regular event at Santa Fe High School until 1995 when two families, one Mormon, one Roman Catholic, complained about the practice. Believing that forcing their children to listen to these prayers was unconstitutional, the parents went to court to have the prayers stopped. The two families both used the name Doe in the court cases to protect themselves from being harassed for bringing the lawsuit.

Santa Fe School Responds Quickly

The first court to hear the case, the U.S. District Court, ruled in the parents' favor. Forcing students to participate in a religious exercise was in violation of the First Amendment. The court ordered the school to stop holding prayers at football games as well as at graduation and other school events. It required the school to bring its policies in line with the Constitution.

The school district was dissatisfied with the order. Its response was twofold. First, the district developed a series of new policies. One of these stated that each school year, the students of Santa Fe High would vote on whether there should be a prayer before each game and, if so, which student would recite it. In this way, the prayer would be a student-sponsored event, elected by a majority of the student body, and not a religious observance imposed by the government.

Second, the school district appealed the court decision to the Court of Appeals. The Court of Appeals agreed with the lower court and held that even the modified policy was a violation of the First Amendment. The school district then appealed the case to the U.S. Supreme Court. On March 29, 2000, the Supreme Court heard arguments from both sides in the dispute.

Arguments for the School District

1. The prayer was given by a student elected by other students, not by a representative of the school, and therefore it was not a matter of the school imposing religion on students.

2. Unlike in the classroom, students are not required to attend the game, so the school is not forcing any religious beliefs or practices on them.

Arguments for the Families

1. The school sponsors the football games. A prayer sent over the school's public address system, by a speaker representing the student body, under the supervision of teachers at the school, and under a school policy, is a government imposition of religion.

2. Football games may not be a required activity for all students, but they are required for members of the band, members of the team, and cheerleaders. In addition, football is a major school activity and an important part of the high school experience. No student should be forced to stay away because of a religious ceremony, and no student should be forced to listen to a religious ceremony.

Conclusion

In June 2000 the Supreme Court issued a ruling in this case. What are the constitutional and legal issues raised by this case? Suppose you were writing the Court's opinion. In whose favor would you decide—the school district's or the families'? What changes in the facts might make your decision different? What if this were not a prayer, but a political speech? What if the student led a moment of silence, instead of a prayer?

The Annotated Constitution

The Preamble of the Constitution begins with the famous words, "We the people of the United States . . . ," emphasizing that under the Constitution, all power comes from the people. Two hundred years after it was written, the Constitution remains the law of the land and a model that other nations have copied.

The Constitution has continued to be a vital and relevant guide to government for more than two centuries because the Framers concentrated on general principles and basic freedoms. By doing so, they ensured that the Constitution would not become mired in detail that would render it unworkable after a few decades.

A complete copy of the U.S. Constitution is reproduced in this chapter. The titles, sections, and clauses are not part of the original document. They have been added to help you find specific information. Some phrases and lines are crossed out because they have been changed by amendments or because they no longer apply. Annotations, or explanations, appear in the margins. Words in **boldface** can be found in the Glossary.

During the past 200 years, six proposed amendments were submitted to the states, but failed to receive ratification. They concerned the following subjects:

- Dividing seats in the House among the states (1789)
- Revoking the citizenship of any American who accepted a title or honor from a foreign government (1810)
- Prohibiting any future amendment concerning slavery (1861)
- Giving the federal government the power to regulate child labor (1924)
- Guaranteeing women equal rights under the law (1972)
- Giving the District of Columbia seats in Congress (1978)

> **PRIMARY SOURCES**
>
> *"[We have created] a republic, if we can keep it."*
> —*Ben Franklin*

E PLURIBUS UNUM

The Constitution of the United States of America

Preamble

We the people of the United States, in order to form a more perfect union, establish justice, insure domestic tranquility, provide for the common defense, promote the general welfare, and secure the blessings of liberty to ourselves and our posterity, do ordain and establish this Constitution for the United States of America.

The Preamble is an introductory statement that sets the tone of the Constitution and sets forth its goals.

The Preamble was written last, after all other parts of the Constitution were decided.

Article I Legislative Branch

Section 1 Two-House Legislature

All legislative powers herein granted shall be vested in a Congress of the United States, which shall consist of a Senate and House of Representatives.

The power to make laws is given to the Senate and the House of Representatives.

Section 2 House of Representatives

1. The House of Representatives shall be composed of members chosen every second year by the people of the several states, and the electors in each state shall have the qualifications requisite for electors of the most numerous branch of the state legislature.

House members are elected every two years by people qualified to vote for members of the largest house of their state legislature.

2. No person shall be a representative who shall not have attained to the age of twenty-five years, and been seven years a citizen of the United States, and who shall not, when elected, be an inhabitant of that state in which he shall be chosen.

House members must be at least twenty-five years old, U.S. citizens for seven years, and residents of the states that elect them.

3. Representatives and direct taxes shall be apportioned among the several states which may be included within this Union, according to their respective numbers, which shall be determined by adding to the whole number of free persons, including those bound to service for a term of years, and

The number of representatives allowed each state depends on the state's population.

Known as the "three-fifths compromise," this provision settled the question of how slaves were to be counted. Since Amendment 13 abolished slavery, it no longer applies.

The population of the states is determined by a federal census taken every ten years.

The first census was taken in 1790.

The governor of the state calls special elections to fill vacancies in that state's representation.

The House chooses its own officers. It alone has the power to accuse a government official of a crime.

Each state is allowed two senators.
Senators are now elected directly.

Senate elections are arranged so that one third of the senators are elected every two years for six-year terms.
Originally, vacancies in the Senate were filled by the state legislature. This process was changed by Amendment 17.

Senators must be at least thirty years old, United States citizens for at least nine years, and residents of the states that elect them.

The Vice President is president of the Senate but only votes to break ties.

excluding Indians not taxed, three fifths of all other persons. The actual enumeration shall be made within three years after the first meeting of the Congress of the United States, and within every subsequent term of ten years, in such manner as they shall by law direct. The number of representatives shall not exceed one for every thirty thousand, but each state shall have at least one representative; and until such enumeration shall be made, the state of New Hampshire shall be entitled to choose 3, Massachusetts 8, Rhode Island and Providence Plantations 1, Connecticut 5, New York 6, New Jersey 4, Pennsylvania 8, Delaware 1, Maryland 6, Virginia 10, North Carolina 5, South Carolina 5, and Georgia 3.

4. When vacancies happen in the representation from any state, the executive authority thereof shall issue writs of election to fill such vacancies.

5. The House of Representatives shall choose their speaker and other officers; and shall have the sole power of **impeachment.**

Section 3 The Senate

1. The Senate of the United States shall be composed of two senators from each state, chosen by the legislature thereof, for six years; and each senator shall have one vote.

2. Immediately after they shall be assembled in consequence of the first election, they shall be divided as equally as may be into three classes. The seats of the senators of the first class shall be vacated at the expiration of the second year, of the second class at the expiration of the fourth year, and of the third class at the expiration of the sixth year, so that one third may be chosen every second year; and if vacancies happen by resignation, or otherwise, during the recess of the legislature of any state, the executive thereof may make temporary appointments until the next meeting of the legislature, which shall then fill such vacancies.

3. No person shall be a senator who shall not have attained to the age of thirty years, and been nine years a citizen of the United States, and who shall not, when elected, be an inhabitant of that state for which he shall be chosen.

4. The Vice President of the United States shall be president of the Senate, but shall have no vote, unless they be equally divided.

5. The Senate shall choose their other officers, and also a president pro tempore, in the absence of the Vice President, or when he shall exercise the office of President of the United States.

The Senate elects its own officers, including a temporary president if needed.

6. The Senate shall have the sole power to try all impeachments. When sitting for that purpose, they shall be on oath or affirmation. When the President of the United States is tried, the chief justice shall preside; and no person shall be convicted without the concurrence of two thirds of the members present.

The Senate tries all impeachment cases. A two-thirds vote is necessary for conviction.

7. Judgment in cases of impeachment shall not extend further than to removal from office, and disqualification to hold and enjoy any office of honor, trust, or profit under the United States; but the party convicted shall, nevertheless, be liable and subject to indictment, trial, judgment, and punishment, according to law.

The Senate can remove from office those officials it convicts on impeachment charges, but any further punishment must come by way of trial in regular courts of law.

Section 4 Elections and Meetings

1. The times, places, and manner of holding elections for senators and representatives shall be prescribed in each state by the legislature thereof; but the Congress may at any time by law make or alter such regulations, except as to the places of choosing senators.

Election regulations are left to the states, though Congress may pass certain laws concerning elections.

2. The Congress shall assemble at least once in every year, and such meeting shall be on the first Monday in December, unless they shall by law appoint a different day.

Congress must meet at least once a year.
Amendment 20 sets January 3 as the date for a session to begin.

Section 5 Rules and Procedures

1. Each House shall be the judge of the elections, returns, and qualifications of its own members, and a majority of each shall constitute a quorum to do business; but a smaller number may adjourn from day to day, and may be authorized to compel the attendance of absent members, in such manner, and under such penalties, as each House may provide.

Each house of Congress has the right to judge the elections and qualifications of its members. To conduct official business, each house must have a majority of its members present.

2. Each House may determine the rules of its proceedings, punish its members from disorderly behavior, and, with the concurrence of two thirds, expel a member.

Each house may make rules for its members. Members may be expelled by a two-thirds vote.

3. Each House shall keep a journal of its proceedings, and from time to time publish the same, excepting such parts as may in their judgment require secrecy;

Each house of Congress must keep and publish a record of its activities.

Neither house may suspend the session for more than three days or move it to a different location without the permission of the other house.

Members of Congress are paid a salary. With certain exceptions, members cannot be sued or arrested for anything they say in Congress.

Members of Congress may not hold any other federal office while serving in Congress.

All money bills must begin in the House. The Senate may change such bills.

A bill passed by both houses of Congress goes to the President. If the President approves the bill, it becomes a law. If the President vetoes a bill, it goes back to Congress. Congress may pass a bill into law over the President's veto by a two-thirds vote.

The veto and the override are examples of the checks and balances built into the federal government.

and the yeas and nays of the members of either House on any question shall, at the desire of one fifth of those present, be entered on the journal.

4. Neither House, during the session of Congress, shall, without the consent of the other, adjourn for more than three days, nor to any other place than that in which the two Houses shall be sitting.

Section 6 Privileges and Restrictions

1. The senators and representatives shall receive a compensation for their services, to be ascertained by law, and paid out of the Treasury of the United States. They shall in all cases, except treason, felony, and breach of the peace, be privileged from arrest during their attendance at the session of their respective houses, and in going to and returning from the same; and for any speech or debate in either house, they shall not be questioned in any other place.

2. No senator or representative shall, during the time for which he was elected, be appointed to any civil office under the authority of the United States, which shall have been created, or the emoluments whereof shall have been increased during such time; and no person holding any office under the United States shall be a member of either house during his continuance in office.

Section 7 Lawmaking Process

1. All bills for raising revenue shall originate in the House of Representatives; but the Senate may propose or concur with amendments as on other bills.

2. Every bill which shall have passed the House of Representatives and the Senate shall, before it becomes a law, be presented to the President of the United States; if he approves he shall sign it, but if not he shall return it with his objections to that house in which it shall have originated, who shall enter the objections at large on their journal, and proceed to reconsider it. If after such reconsideration two thirds of that house shall agree to pass the bill, it shall be sent, together with the objections, to the other house, by which it shall likewise be reconsidered, and if approved by two thirds of that house, it shall become a law. But in all such cases the votes of both houses shall be determined by yeas and nays, and the names of the persons voting for and against the

bill shall be entered on the journal of each house respectively. If any bill shall not be returned by the President within ten days (Sundays excepted) after it shall have been presented to him, the same shall be a law, in like manner as if he had signed it, unless the Congress by their adjournment prevent its return, in which case it shall not be a law.

A bill becomes a law if the President holds it unsigned for ten days, unless Congress adjourns in the meantime.

3. Every order, resolution, or vote to which the concurrence of the Senate and House of Representatives may be necessary (except on a question of adjournment) shall be presented to the President of the United States; and before the same shall take effect, shall be approved by him, or being disapproved by him, shall be repassed by two thirds of the Senate and House of Representatives, according to the rules and limitations prescribed in the case of a bill.

Every order or resolution of Congress should be presented to the President. *Actually, many congressional resolutions do not go to the President. But any bill that is to become a law must be sent to the President.*

Section 8 Powers Granted to Congress

The Congress shall have power:

CONGRESS HAS THE POWER TO:

1. To lay and collect taxes, duties, imposts, and excises, to pay the debts and provide for the common defense and general welfare of the United States; but all duties, imposts, and excises shall be uniform throughout the United States;

collect taxes and pay debts; provide for the defense and welfare of the United States;

2. To borrow money on the credit of the United States;

borrow money;

3. To regulate commerce with foreign nations, and among the several states, and with the Indian tribes;

regulate trade;

4. To establish a uniform rule of naturalization, and uniform laws on the subject of bankruptcies throughout the United States;

establish laws concerning citizenship and **bankruptcy,** the inability to pay one's debts;

5. To coin money, regulate the value thereof, and of foreign coin, and fix the standard of weights and measures;

coin money and establish standards of weights and measures;

6. To provide for the punishment of counterfeiting the securities and current coin of the United States;

determine the punishment for counterfeiting money;

7. To establish post offices and post roads;

build post offices and roads;

8. To promote the progress of science and useful arts by securing for limited times to authors and inventors the exclusive right to their respective writings and discoveries;

issue copyrights and patents;

9. To constitute tribunals inferior to the Supreme Court;

set up federal courts;

10. To define and punish piracies and felonies committed on the high seas, and offenses against the law of nations;

punish crimes committed against ships at sea;

declare war and determine the treatment for prisoners of war;

maintain an army;

maintain a navy;

make regulations for the armed forces;

provide for calling out the national guard to handle emergencies;

maintain and train the national guard;

make laws for the District of Columbia and other federal properties;
To win southern support for his economic plan in 1790, Alexander Hamilton supported a southern city, Washington, D.C., as the capital.

make all laws "necessary and proper."
Known as the elastic clause, it allows Congress to make laws not specifically mentioned in the Constitution.

CONGRESS CANNOT:

This clause, referring to the slave trade until 1808, no longer applies.

illegally imprison people;

11. To declare war, ~~grant letters of marque and reprisal,~~ and make rules concerning captures on land and water;

12. To raise and support armies; but no appropriation of money to that use shall be for a longer term than two years;

13. To provide and maintain a navy;

14. To make rules for the government and regulation of the land and naval forces;

15. To provide for calling forth the militia to execute the laws of the union, suppress insurrections, and repel invasions;

16. To provide for organizing, arming, and disciplining the militia, and for governing such part of them as may be employed in the service of the United States, reserving to the states respectively the appointment of the officers and the authority of training the militia according to the discipline prescribed by Congress;

17. To exercise exclusive legislation in all cases whatsoever over such district—not exceeding ten miles square—as may, by cession of particular states, and the acceptance of Congress, become the seat of the government of the United States, and to exercise like authority over all places purchased by the consent of the legislature of the state in which the same shall be for the erection of forts, magazines, arsenals, dockyards, and other needful buildings; and

18. To make all laws which shall be necessary and proper for carrying into execution the foregoing powers and all other powers vested by this Constitution in the government of the United States, or in any department or officer thereof.

Section 9 Powers Denied to the Federal Government

1. ~~The migration or importation of such persons as any of the states now existing shall think proper to admit shall not be prohibited by the Congress prior to the year one thousand eight hundred and eight, but a tax or duty may be imposed on such importation, not exceeding ten dollars for each person.~~

2. The privilege of the **writ of habeas corpus** shall not be suspended, unless when in cases of rebellion or invasion the public safety may require it.

3. No **bill of attainder** or **ex post facto** law shall be passed.

4. No capitation or other direct tax shall be laid, unless in proportion to the census or enumeration herein before directed to be taken.

5. No tax or duty shall be laid on articles exported from any state.

6. No preference shall be given by any regulation of commerce or revenue to the ports of one state over those of another; nor shall vessels bound to or from one state be obliged to enter, clear, or pay duties in another.

7. No money shall be drawn from the Treasury, but in consequence of appropriations made by law; and a regular statement and account of the receipts and expenditures of all public money shall be published from time to time.

8. No title of nobility shall be granted by the United States; and no person holding any office of profit or trust under them shall, without the consent of the Congress, accept of any present, emolument, office, or title of any kind whatever from any king, prince, or foreign state.

Section 10 Powers Denied to the States

1. No state shall enter into any treaty, alliance, or confederation; grant letters of marque and reprisal; coin money; emit bills of credit; make anything but gold and silver coin a tender in payment of debts; pass any bill of attainder, *ex post facto* law, or law impairing the obligation of contracts, or grant any title of nobility.

2. No state shall, without the consent of Congress, lay any imposts or duties on imports or exports, except what may be absolutely necessary for executing its inspection laws; and the net produce of all duties and imposts laid by any state on imports or exports shall be for the use of the Treasury of the United States; and all such laws shall be subject to the revision and control of the Congress.

3. No state shall, without the consent of Congress, lay any duty of tonnage, keep troops, or ships of war in time of peace, enter into any agreement or compact with another state, or with a foreign power, or engage in war, unless actually invaded, or in such imminent danger as will not admit of delay.

pass laws of unfair punishment;

pass any direct tax unless it is in proportion to population;
An exception is the income tax, established by Amendment 16.

tax exports;

pass any law that would favor the trade of a particular state;

spend money that has not been authorized by law;

grant any title of nobility; government officials may not accept gifts or titles from other nations unless Congress approves.

STATE GOVERNMENTS CANNOT:

make treaties or alliances; coin money; give bills of credit; pass laws of unfair punishment; grant titles of nobility;

tax imports or exports without the consent of Congress;

tax ships without the consent of Congress; keep a regular army; make agreements with other states or with foreign countries; or engage in war, unless invaded or in grave danger.

Article II Executive Branch

Section 1 President and Vice President

The President is the chief executive, who holds office with the Vice President for a four-year term.

The President is elected by an electoral college made up of electors appointed by the states. The number of electors each state may have is equal to the number of its senators and representatives.

This method of electing a President and Vice President was changed by Amendment 12.

1. The executive power shall be vested in a President of the United States of America. He shall hold his office during the term of four years, and together with the Vice President, chosen for the same term, be elected as follows:

2. Each state shall appoint, in such manner as the legislature thereof may direct, a number of electors equal to the whole number of senators and representatives to which the state may be entitled in the Congress; but no senator or representative, or person holding an office of trust or profit under the United States, shall be appointed an elector.

3. ~~The electors shall meet in their respective states, and vote by ballot for two persons, of whom one at least shall not be an inhabitant of the same state with themselves. And they shall make a list of all persons voted for, and of the number of votes for each; which list they shall sign and certify, and transmit sealed to the seat of the government of the United States, directed to the president of the Senate. The president of the Senate shall, in the presence of the Senate and House of Representatives, open all the certificates, and the votes shall then be counted. The person having the greatest number of votes shall be the President, if such number be a majority of the whole number of electors appointed; and if there be more than one who have such a majority, and have an equal number of votes, then the House of Representatives shall immediately choose by ballot one of them for President; and if no person have a majority, then from the five highest on the list the said house shall in like manner choose the President. But in choosing the President, the votes shall be taken by states, the representation from each state having one vote; a quorum for this purpose shall consist of a member or members from two thirds of the states, and a majority of all the states shall be necessary to a choice. In every case, after the choice of the President, the person having the greatest number of votes of the electors shall be the Vice President. But if there should remain two or more who have equal votes, the Senate shall choose from them by ballot the Vice President.~~

Congress decides when electors are chosen and when they will vote.

4. The Congress may determine the time of choosing the electors, and the day on which they shall give their votes; which day shall be the same throughout the United States.

5. No person except a natural-born citizen ~~or a citizen of the United States at the time of the adoption of this Constitution,~~ shall be eligible to the office of President; neither shall any person be eligible to that office who shall not have attained to the age of thirty-five years and been fourteen years a resident within the United States.

6. In case of the removal of the President from office, or of his death, resignation, or inability to discharge the powers and duties of the said office, the same shall devolve on the Vice President, and the Congress may by law provide for the case of removal, death, resignation, or inability, both of the President and Vice President, declaring what officer shall then act as President, and such officer shall act accordingly, until the disability be removed, or a President shall be elected.

7. The President shall at stated times receive for his services a compensation, which shall neither be increased nor diminished during the period for which he shall have been elected, and he shall not receive within that period any other emolument from the United States, or any of them.

8. Before he enter on the execution of his office, he shall take the following **oath** or affirmation: "I do solemnly swear (or affirm) that I will faithfully execute the office of President of the United States, and will to the best of my ability, preserve, protect, and defend the Constitution of the United States."

Section 2 Powers of the President

1. The President shall be commander in chief of the army and navy of the United States, and of the militia of the several states, when called into the actual service of the United States; he may require the opinion in writing of the principal officer in each of the executive departments upon any subject relating to the duties of their respective offices, and he shall have power to grant reprieves and pardons for offenses against the United States, except in cases of impeachment.

2. He shall have power, by and with the advice and consent of the Senate, to make treaties, provided two thirds of the senators present concur; and he shall nominate and, by and with the advice and consent of the Senate, shall appoint ambassadors, other public ministers and consuls, judges of the Supreme Court, and all other officers of the United States whose appointments are not herein otherwise

The President must be a natural-born citizen of the United States, at least 35 years old, and a resident of the United States for at least 14 years.

This section has been modified by Amendment 25.

The President receives a salary, which cannot be lowered or raised during his term in office.

Before taking office, the President swears to uphold and defend the Constitution.

The President is commander in chief of the armed forces.

The President can grant delays of punishment and pardons for offenses against the United States, except in impeachment cases.

The President has the power to make treaties and to appoint ambassadors and other officers. The Senate must approve such appointments. Minor appointments may be made without Senate approval.

When the Senate is not in session, the President may make temporary appointments to office.

The President is required to report to Congress annually on the condition of the nation, to receive ambassadors, and to carry out the laws. He also has the power to call special sessions of Congress and to adjourn Congress if necessary.

The President, Vice President, and other government officials, such as federal judges and Cabinet members, can be forced from office for major offenses (**high crimes**) and certain minor offenses (**misdemeanors**).

The right to decide legal cases is given to a Supreme Court and other lesser courts authorized by Congress. Federal judges can hold office for life if they are not **impeached** and found guilty of certain crimes.

The federal courts try all cases involving the Constitution, federal laws, and treaties. Lawsuits involving the federal government, two states, or citizens of different states are tried in federal courts.

provided for, and which shall be established by law; but the Congress may by law vest the appointment of such inferior officers as they think proper in the President alone, in the courts of law, or in the heads of departments.

3. The President shall have power to fill up all vacancies that may happen during the recess of the Senate, by granting commissions which shall expire at the end of their next session.

Section 3 Duties of the President

He shall from time to time give to the Congress information of the state of the Union, and recommend to their consideration such measures as he shall judge necessary and expedient; he may, on extraordinary occasions, convene both houses, or either of them, and in case of disagreement between them with respect to the time of adjournment, he may adjourn them to such time as he shall think proper; he shall receive ambassadors and other public ministers; he shall take care that the laws be faithfully executed, and shall commission all the officers of the United States.

Section 4 Impeachment and Removal From Office

The President, Vice President, and all civil officers of the United States shall be removed from office on impeachment for, and conviction of, treason, bribery, or other high crimes and misdemeanors.

Article III Judicial Branch

Section 1 The Federal Courts

The judicial power of the United States shall be vested in one Supreme Court, and in such inferior courts as the Congress may from time to time ordain and establish. The judges, both of the Supreme and inferior courts, shall hold their offices during good behavior and shall at stated times receive for their services a compensation, which shall not be diminished during their continuance in office.

Section 2 Jurisdiction of the Federal Courts

1. The judicial power shall extend to all cases in law and equity arising under this Constitution, the laws of the United States, and treaties made, or which

shall be made, under their authority; to all cases affecting ambassadors, other public ministers and consuls; to all cases of admiralty and maritime jurisdiction; to controversies to which the United States shall be a party; to controversies between two or more states; ~~between a state and citizens of another state;~~ between citizens of different states; between citizens of the same state claiming lands under grants of different states, and between a state, or the citizens thereof, and foreign states, citizens, or subjects.

Amendment 11 changed this part.

2. In all cases affecting ambassadors, other public ministers and consuls, and those in which a state shall be a party, the Supreme Court shall have original jurisdiction. In all the other cases before mentioned, the Supreme Court shall have appellate jurisdiction, both as to law and fact, with such exceptions, and under such regulations as the Congress shall make.

Cases involving ambassadors or officials of foreign nations or those involving states are tried in the Supreme Court. Other cases begin in lower courts but may be appealed to the Supreme Court.

3. The trial of all crimes, except in cases of impeachment, shall be by jury; and such trial shall be held in the state where the said crimes shall have been committed; but when not committed within any state, the trial shall be at such place or places as the Congress may by law have directed.

All crimes, except in cases of impeachment, shall be tried by jury.

Section 3 Treason

1. Treason against the United States shall consist only in levying war against them, or in adhering to their enemies, giving them aid and comfort. No person shall be convicted of treason, unless on the testimony of two witnesses to the same overt act or on confession in open court.

It is considered an act of treason to wage war against the United States or to give aid to its enemies.

2. The Congress shall have power to declare the punishment of treason, but no attainder of treason shall work corruption of blood, or forfeiture except during the life of the person attained.

Congress may decide the punishment for traitors, but it may not punish the families of convicted traitors by taking away their civil rights or property.

Article IV The States and the Federal Government

Section 1 State Records

Full faith and credit shall be given in each state to the public acts, records, and judicial proceedings of every other state. And the Congress may by general laws prescribe the manner in which such acts, records, and proceedings shall be proved, and the effect thereof.

The official acts (such as issuing marriage certificates) of one state must be recognized as legal by all other states.

States must treat citizens of another state as fairly as their own citizens.

Courts have, however, allowed states to give residents certain privileges, such as lower tuition rates at state schools.

A state governor may demand the return of a criminal who has fled to another state.

*The act of returning a suspected criminal or an escaped prisoner to the state where he or she is wanted is called **extradition.***

This provision for the return of runaway slaves has had no effect since Amendment 13 abolished slavery in 1865.

Congress has the power to admit new states to the Union.

Congress has the power to make rules for managing and governing land owned by the United States, such as territories and federal lands within a state.

The federal government guarantees to each state a **republican** form of government, protection against invasion, and protection against disturbances within the state.

The Constitution can be **amended,** or changed, if necessary in the following ways: an amendment can be proposed

Section 2 Privileges and Immunities of Citizens

1. The citizens of each state shall be entitled to all privileges and immunities of citizens in the several states.

2. A person charged in any state with treason, felony, or other crime, who shall flee from justice and be found in another state, shall, on demand of the executive authority of the state from which he fled, be delivered up to be removed to the state, having jurisdiction of the crime.

3. ~~No person held to service or labor in one state, under the laws thereof, escaping into another shall, in consequence of any law or regulation therein, be discharged from such service or labor, but shall be delivered up on claim of the party to whom such service or labor may be due.~~

Section 3 New States and Territories

1. New states may be admitted by the Congress into this Union; but no new state shall be formed or erected within the jurisdiction of any other state; nor any state be formed by the junction of two or more states, or parts of states, without the consent of the legislatures of the states concerned, as well as of the Congress.

2. The Congress shall have power to dispose of and make all needful rules and regulations respecting the territory or other property belonging to the United States; and nothing in this Constitution shall be so construed as to prejudice any claims of the United States, or of any particular state.

Section 4 Guarantees to the States

The United States shall guarantee to every state in this union a republican form of government, and shall protect each of them against invasion; and on application of the legislature, or of the executive—when the legislature cannot be convened—against domestic violence.

Article V Amending the Constitution

The Congress, whenever two thirds of both houses shall deem it necessary, shall propose amendments to this Constitution or, on the application of the legislatures of two thirds of the several states, shall call a convention for proposing amendments, which in either case shall be valid to all intents and purposes as part of this Constitution when ratified by the legislatures of three fourths of the several states, or by conventions in three fourths thereof, as the one or the other mode of ratification may be proposed by the Congress; provided that ~~no amendment which may be made prior to the year one thousand eight hundred and eight shall in any manner affect the first and fourth clauses in the ninth section of the first article, and that~~ no state, without its consent, shall be deprived of its equal suffrage in the Senate.

by a two-thirds vote of both houses of Congress or by a national convention called by two-thirds of the states. Amendments must be ratified, or approved, by three fourths of the state legislatures or by special conventions in three fourths of the states. Congress decides which method will be used.

This clause ceased to apply in 1808.

Article VI General Provisions

1. All debts contracted and engagements entered into before the adoption of this Constitution shall be as valid against the United States under this Constitution as under the Confederation.

All money previously borrowed under the Articles of Confederation will be repaid under the Constitution.

2. This Constitution, and the laws of the United States which shall be made in pursuance thereof; and all treaties made, or which shall be made, under the authority of the United States, shall be the supreme law of the land; and the judges in every state shall be bound thereby, anything in the constitution or laws of any state to the contrary notwithstanding.

The Constitution, federal laws, and the treaties of the United States are the supreme law of the land, and thus outweigh state laws.

3. The senators and representatives before mentioned, and the members of the several state legislatures, and all executive and judicial officers, both of the United States and of the several states, shall be bound by oath or affirmation, to support this Constitution; but no religious test shall ever be required as a qualification to any office or public trust under the United States.

All federal and state officials must take an oath of office promising to support the Constitution. There can be no religious requirement for holding office.

This clause emphasizes the separation of church and state.

Article VII Ratification of the Constitution

The ratification of the conventions of nine states shall be sufficient for the establishment of this Constitution between the states so ratifying the same.

The Constitution will take effect when it is approved by nine states.

The Constitution went into effect on March 4, 1789.

Signing the Constitution

Done in convention, by the unanimous consent of the states present, the seventeenth day of September, in the year of our Lord one thousand seven hundred and eighty-seven, and of the independence of the United States of America the twelfth. In witness whereof, we have hereunto subscribed our names.

Attest: William Jackson
Secretary

George Washington
President and deputy from Virginia

New Hampshire
John Langdon
Nicholas Gilman

Massachusetts
Nathaniel Gorham
Rufus King

Connecticut
William Samuel Johnson
Roger Sherman

New York
Alexander Hamilton

New Jersey
William Livingston
David Brearley
William Paterson
Jonathan Dayton

Pennsylvania
Benjamin Franklin
Thomas Mifflin
Robert Morris
George Clymer
Thomas FitzSimmons
Jared Ingersoll
James Wilson
Gouverneur Morris

Delaware
George Read
Gunning Bedford, Jr.
John Dickinson
Richard Bassett
Jacob Broom

Maryland
James McHenry
Dan of St. Thomas Jennifer
Daniel Carroll

Virginia
John Blair
James Madison, Jr.

North Carolina
William Blount
Richard Dobbs Spaight
Hugh Williamson

South Carolina
John Rutledge
Charles Cotesworth Pinckney
Charles Pinckney
Pierce Butler

Georgia
William Few
Abraham Baldwin

Amendments to the Constitution

Amendment 1 (1791)

Freedoms of Speech, Press, Assembly, and Petition. Congress shall make no law respecting an establishment of religion, or prohibiting the free exercise thereof; or **abridging** the freedom of speech, or of the press; or the right of the people peaceably to assemble, and to **petition** the government for a **redress** of **grievances.**

Amendment 2 (1791)

Right to Bear Arms. A well-regulated militia being necessary to the security of a free state, the right of the people to keep and bear arms shall not be infringed.

Amendment 3 (1791)

Lodging Troops in Private Homes. No soldier shall, in time of peace, be quartered in any house without the consent of the owner, nor in time of war, but in a manner to be prescribed by law.

Amendment 4 (1791)

Search and Seizure. The right of the people to be secure in their persons, houses, papers, and effects against unreasonable searches and seizures shall not be violated, and no warrants shall issue but upon probable cause, supported by oath or affirmation, and particularly describing the place to be searched and the persons or things to be seized.

Amendment 5 (1791)

Rights of the Accused. No person shall be held to answer for a capital or otherwise infamous crime, unless on a presentment or indictment of a grand jury, except in cases arising in the land or naval forces, or in the militia, when in actual service in time of war or public danger; nor shall any person be subject for the same offense to be twice put in jeopardy of life or limb; nor shall be compelled in any criminal case to be a witness against himself, nor be deprived of life, liberty, or property without due process of law; nor shall private property be taken for public use without just compensation.

Amendment 6 (1791)

Right to a Speedy Trial. In all criminal prosecutions the accused shall enjoy the right to a speedy and public trial by an impartial jury of the state and district wherein the crime shall have been committed, which

The first ten amendments are known as the Bill of Rights. The dates on which these and other amendments were declared ratified are given in parentheses.

Congress may not make laws interfering with the freedoms of religion, speech, the press, assembly, and petition.

The states have the right to maintain national guard units.

Troops cannot be lodged in private homes during peacetime.

People are protected against unreasonable searches and arrests.

A person cannot be tried for a **capital crime** (a crime punishable by death) unless charged by a grand jury, be tried twice for the same crime, nor be forced to testify against himself or herself. A person may not be deprived of life, liberty, or property except by lawful means. The government must pay a fair price for property taken for public use.

A person accused of a crime has a right to a speedy public trial by jury, to information about the accusation, to help from the court in bringing favorable witnesses to the trial, and to the aid of a lawyer.

In civil lawsuits involving more than $20, the right to a jury trial is guaranteed.

An appeals court cannot change a verdict because it disagrees with the decision of the jury. It can set aside a verdict only if legal errors have been made.

Bails, fines, and punishments cannot be unreasonable.

The basic rights of the people, even those not specified in the Constitution, cannot be denied.

The powers not given to the federal government are to be held by the states or by the people.

Federal courts do not have the power to hear suits brought against a state by the citizens of another state or by foreigners.

A citizen can, however, sue a state government in a state court.

The members of the electoral college vote for the President and Vice President on separate ballots. If no person receives a majority of the electoral votes for President, the House of Representatives elects the President. In such an election the representatives from each state have one vote among them. A majority of these votes is necessary to elect the President.

district shall have been previously ascertained by law, and to be informed of the nature and cause of the accusation; to be confronted with the witnesses against him; to have compulsory process for obtaining witnesses in his favor, and to have the assistance of counsel for his defense.

Amendment 7 (1791)

Trial by Jury in Civil Cases. In suits at common law, where the value in controversy shall exceed twenty dollars, the right of trial by jury shall be preserved, and no fact tried by a jury shall be otherwise reexamined in any court of the United States than according to the rules of the common law.

Amendment 8 (1791)

Bail and Punishment. Excessive bail shall not be required, nor excessive fines imposed, nor cruel and unusual punishments inflicted.

Amendment 9 (1791)

Powers Reserved for the People. The enumeration in the Constitution of certain rights shall not be construed to deny or disparage others retained by the people.

Amendment 10 (1791)

Powers Reserved for the States. The powers not delegated to the United States by the Constitution, nor prohibited by it to the states, are reserved to the states respectively, or to the people.

Amendment 11 (1795)

Suits Against States. The judicial power of the United States shall not be construed to extend to any suit in law or equity, commenced or prosecuted against one of the United States by citizens of another state, or by citizens or subjects of any foreign state.

Amendment 12 (1804)

Election of Chief Executives. The electors shall meet in their respective states and vote by ballot for President and Vice President, one of whom at least shall not be an inhabitant of the same state with themselves; they shall name in their ballots the person voted for as President, and in distinct ballots the person voted for as Vice President, and they shall make distinct lists of all persons voted for as President, and of all persons voted for as Vice President, and of the number of votes for each, which lists they shall sign and certify, and transmit sealed to the seat of the government of the United States, directed to the president of the Senate; the president of the Senate shall, in the presence of the Senate and House of Representatives, open all the certificates, and the votes shall then be counted; the person having the greatest number of votes for President shall be President, if such number be a majority of the whole number of electors appointed; and if no person have such majority, then from the persons having the highest numbers not exceeding three on the list of those voted for as President the House of Representatives shall choose immediately by ballot the President. But in choosing the President, the votes shall be taken by states, the representation from each state having one vote; a quorum for this purpose shall consist of a member or members from two thirds of the states, and a majority of all the states shall be necessary to a choice. And if the House of Representatives shall not choose a President whenever the right of choice shall devolve upon them, ~~before the fourth day of March next following,~~ then the Vice President shall act as President, as in the case of the death or other constitutional disability of the President. The person having the greatest number of votes as Vice President shall be the Vice President, if such number be a majority of the whole number of electors appointed; and if no person have a majority, then from the two highest numbers on the list the Senate shall choose the Vice President; a quorum for the purpose shall consist of two thirds of the whole number of senators, and a majority of the whole number shall be necessary to a choice. But no person constitutionally ineligible to the office of President shall be eligible to that of Vice President of the United States.

Amendment 13 (1865)

Section 1 Abolition of Slavery. Neither slavery nor involuntary servitude, except as a punishment of crime whereof the party shall have been duly convicted, shall exist within the United States, or any place subject to their jurisdiction.

Section 2 Enforcement. Congress shall have power to enforce this article by appropriate legislation.

Amendment 14 (1868)

Section 1 Definition of Citizenship. All persons born or **naturalized** in the United States and subject to the jurisdiction thereof are citizens of the United States and of the state wherein they reside. No state shall make or enforce any law which shall abridge the privileges or immunities of citizens of the United States; nor shall any state deprive any person of life, liberty, or property without due process

This amendment changed the way the electoral college voted. Previously, each elector voted for two people. The candidate with the most votes became President and the runner-up became Vice President. In 1800, Thomas Jefferson and Aaron Burr received the same number of votes.

The reference to March 4 no longer applies, since the President takes office in January. (Amendment 20)

If no person receives a majority of the votes for Vice President, the Senate elects the Vice President. A majority vote is necessary.

Slavery is prohibited. Congress is given the power to enforce the abolition of slavery.

Congress can pass laws to carry out this amendment.

Citizenship is defined; all citizens are guaranteed equal protection of the law.

This amendment has had important implications for minority groups and immigrants.

Section 2 replaces the "three-fifths" clause and provides that representation in the House be based on a state's population. It further provides that if a state prevents certain citizens from voting, that state's representation in Congress may be reduced.

The penalty provision has never been enforced.

If a federal officeholder goes against the oath of office and rebels against the country or helps its enemies, that person can never again hold a federal office. Congress may, however, allow such a person to hold office if two thirds of both houses agree.

This section was aimed at keeping former Confederate officials from holding public office after the Civil War.

People who had loaned money to the Confederacy during the Civil War would not be repaid.

Congress can pass laws to carry out this amendment.

This amendment gave black men, both former slaves and free blacks, the right to vote.

Congress can make laws to carry out this amendment.

of law; nor deny to any person within its jurisdiction the equal protection of the laws.

Section 2 Apportionment of Representatives. Representatives shall be apportioned among the several states according to their respective numbers, counting the whole number of persons in each state ~~excluding Indians not taxed.~~ But when the right to vote at any election for the choice of electors for President and Vice President of the United States, representatives in Congress, the executive and judicial officers of a state, or the members of the legislature thereof, is denied to any of the ~~male~~ inhabitants of such state, being ~~twenty-one years of age and~~ citizens of the United States, or in any way abridged, except for participation in rebellion or other crime, the basis of representation therein shall be reduced in the proportion which the number of such ~~male~~ citizens shall bear to the whole number of ~~male~~ citizens ~~twenty-one years of age~~ in such state.

Section 3 Penalty for Participating in Rebellion. No person shall be a senator or representative in Congress, or elector of President and Vice President, or hold any office, civil or military, under the United States, or under any state, who having previously taken an oath as a member of Congress, or as an officer of the United States, or as a member of any state legislature, or as an executive or judicial officer of any state, to support the Constitution of the United States, shall have engaged in insurrection or rebellion against the same, or given aid or comfort to the enemies thereof. But Congress may by a vote of two thirds of each house, remove such disability.

Section 4 Confederate Debt. The validity of the public debt of the United States, authorized by law, including debts incurred for payments of pensions and bounties for services in suppressing insurrection or rebellion, shall not be questioned. But neither the United States nor any state shall assume or pay any debt or obligation incurred in aid of insurrection or rebellion against the United States, ~~or any claim for the loss or emancipation in any slave;~~ but all such debts, obligations, and claims shall be held illegal and void.

Section 5 Enforcement. The Congress shall have power to enforce, by appropriate legislation, the provisions of this article.

Amendment 15 (1870)

Section 1 Voting Rights. The right of citizens of the United States to vote shall not be denied or abridged by the United States or by any state on account of race, color, or previous condition of servitude.

Section 2 Enforcement. The Congress shall have power to enforce this article by appropriate legislation.

Amendment 16 (1913)

Income Tax. The Congress shall have power to lay and collect taxes on incomes, from whatever source derived, without apportionment among the several states, and without regard to any census or enumeration.

Congress has the power to tax people's income.

This amendment changes Article I, Section 3, Clause 4.

Amendment 17 (1913)

Direct Election of Senators. The Senate of the United States shall be composed of two senators from each state, elected by the people thereof for six years; and each senator shall have one vote. The electors in each state shall have the qualifications requisite for electors of the most numerous branch of the state legislatures.

Senators are to be elected directly by the voters rather than by state legislatures.

This clause changes Article I, Section 3.

When vacancies happen in the representation of any state in the Senate, the executive authority of such state shall issue writs of election to fill such vacancies, provided that the legislature of any state may empower the executive thereof to make temporary appointments until the people fill the vacancies by election as the legislature may direct.

When a Senate seat becomes vacant, the governor of the state must order an election to fill the seat. The state legislature can allow the governor to fill the seat temporarily until an election is held.

~~This amendment shall not be so construed as to affect the election or term of any senator chosen before it becomes valid as part of the Constitution.~~

Senators who had already been elected by the state were not affected by this amendment.

Amendment 18 (1919)

Section 1 Prohibition. ~~After one year from the ratification of this article the manufacture, sale, or transportation of intoxicating liquors within, the importation thereof into, or the exportation thereof from the United States and all territory subject to the jurisdiction thereof for beverage purposes is hereby prohibited.~~

The manufacture, sale, and transportation of alcoholic beverages was forbidden.

The amendment was repealed, or canceled, by Amendment 21. This amendment and the period during which it was in effect are known as Prohibition.

Section 2 Enforcement. ~~The Congress and the several states shall have concurrent power to enforce this article by appropriate legislation.~~

Both the states and the federal government had the power to pass laws to carry out this amendment.

Section 3 Limited Time for Ratification. ~~This article shall be inoperative unless it shall have been ratified as an amendment to the Constitution by the legislatures of the several states, as provided in the Constitution, within seven years from the date of submission hereof to the states by the Congress.~~

This amendment had to be approved within seven years.

This was the first amendment to include a time limit for ratification.

Amendment 19 (1920)

Section 1 Women's Suffrage. The right of citizens of the United States to vote shall not be denied or abridged by the United States or by any state on account of sex.

Women have the right to vote.

This amendment was ratified in time for women to vote in the presidential election of 1920.

Congress can pass laws to carry out this amendment.

The terms of senators and representatives end on January 3 instead of March 4, and the terms of the President and Vice President end on January 20 rather than March 4.

This is called the "lame duck" amendment. By specifying earlier dates for starting new terms of office, this amendment assured that officials who were defeated in an election would not continue to serve as "lame ducks."

Congress must meet at least once a year, beginning on January 3.

If a President-elect dies before taking office, the Vice President-elect will become President.

If a President-elect is disqualified, the Vice President-elect will serve as President until the President-elect qualifies. Congress may declare who will serve as President if neither the President-elect nor the Vice President-elect qualifies.

Congress can pass laws in cases where a presidential candidate dies while an election is being decided in the House.

The date is set for when this amendment becomes effective.

A time limit for ratification is set.

Amendment 18 is repealed.

Section 2 Enforcement. The Congress shall have power to enforce this article by appropriate legislation.

Amendment 20 (1933)

Section 1 Terms of President, Vice President, and Congress. The terms of the President and Vice President shall end at noon on the 20th day of January, and the terms of senators and representatives at noon on the third day of January, of the years in which such terms would have ended if this article had not been ratified; and the terms of their successors shall then begin.

Section 2 Sessions of Congress. The Congress shall assemble at least once in every year, and such meeting shall begin at noon on the third day of January, unless they shall by law appoint a different day.

Section 3 Presidential Succession. If, at the time fixed for the beginning of the term of the President, the President-elect shall have died, the Vice President-elect shall become President. If a President shall not have been chosen before the time fixed for the beginning of his term, or if the President-elect shall have failed to qualify, then the Vice President-elect shall act as President until a President shall have qualified; and the Congress may by law provide for the case wherein neither a President-elect nor a Vice President-elect shall have qualified, declaring who shall then act as President, or the manner in which one who is to act shall be selected, and such person act accordingly until a President or Vice President shall have qualified.

Section 4 Elections Decided by Congress. The Congress may by law provide for the case of the death of any of the persons from whom the House of Representatives may choose a President whenever the right of choice shall have devolved upon them, and for the case of the death of any of the persons from whom the Senate may choose a Vice President whenever the right of choice shall have devolved upon them.

Section 5 Effective Date. Sections 1 and 2 shall take effect on the 15th of October following the ratification of this article.

Section 6 Limited Time for Ratification. This article shall be inoperative unless it shall have been ratified as an amendment to the Constitution by the legislatures of three fourths of the several states within seven years from the date of its submission.

Amendment 21 (1933)

Section 1 Repeal of Prohibition. The eighteenth article of amendment to the Constitution of the United States is hereby repealed.

Section 2 State Laws. The transportation or importation into any state, territory, or possession of the United States for delivery or use therein of intoxicating liquors in violation of the laws thereof is hereby prohibited.

Each state is free to ban the making and selling of alcoholic beverages within its borders. Bringing liquor into a "dry" state is a federal offense.

Section 3 Conditions for Ratification. ~~This article shall be inoperative unless it shall have been ratified as an amendment to the Constitution by convention in the several states, as provided in the Constitution, within seven years from the date of the submission hereof to the states by the Congress.~~

Special conventions were called, and a time limit set, for ratification.

Amendment 22 (1951)

Section 1 Presidential Term Limits. No person shall be elected to the office of the President more than twice, and no person who has held the office of President, or acted as President, for more than two years of a term to which some other person was elected President shall be elected to the office of the President more than once. ~~But this article shall not apply to any person holding the office of President when this article was proposed by the Congress, and shall not prevent any person who may be holding the office of President, or acting as President, during the term within which this article becomes operative from holding the office of President or acting as President during the remainder of such term.~~

The President is limited to two terms in office.

Until 1940 no President had served more than two terms in office. This amendment was proposed after Franklin D. Roosevelt won a fourth term as President. Roosevelt died early in his fourth term.

Section 2 Time Limit for Ratification. ~~This article shall be inoperative unless it shall have been ratified as an amendment to the Constitution by the legislatures of three-fourths of the several states within seven years from the date of its submission to the states by the Congress.~~

A seven-year time limit was set for ratification.

Amendment 23 (1961)

Section 1 Voting Rights for the District of Columbia. The District constituting the seat of government of the United States shall appoint in such manner as the Congress may direct: A number of electors of President and Vice President equal to the whole number of senators and representatives in Congress to which the district would be entitled if it were a state, but in no event more than the least populous state; they shall be in addition to those appointed by the states, but they shall be considered, for the purposes of the election of President and Vice President, to be electors appointed by a state; and they shall meet in the district and perform such duties as provided by the twelfth article of amendment.

The residents of the District of Columbia are given the right to vote for President and Vice President.

Section 2 Enforcement. The Congress shall have the power to enforce this article by appropriate legislation.

Congress can pass laws to carry out this amendment.

No citizen can be made to pay a tax for the right to vote in a federal election.

In 1966 a Supreme Court case found poll taxes on state elections unconstitutional.

Congress can pass laws to carry out this amendment.

The Vice President becomes President if the President dies or must leave office.

If the office of Vice President is vacant, the President shall appoint and the Congress approve a new Vice President.

If the President declares himself unable to continue as President, the Vice President becomes acting President.

Whenever the Vice President and a majority of other officers declare that the President is disabled, the Vice President becomes acting President.

When the President declares that he is again able, he resumes his duties. But if the Vice President and other officers disagree, Congress decides whether or not the President is able to resume the powers and duties of the office.

Amendment 25 sought a solution to problems that came up in the 1900s when two Presidents—Wilson and Eisenhower—became seriously ill during their terms. To avoid disputes over who should be in control at such times, this amendment spells out the line of responsibility.

Amendment 24 (1964)

Section 1 Abolition of Poll Taxes. The right of citizens of the United States to vote in any primary or other election for President or Vice President, for electors for President or Vice President, or for senator or representative in Congress, shall not be denied or abridged by the United States or any state by reason of failure to pay any poll tax or other tax.

Section 2 Enforcement. The Congress shall have the power to enforce this article by appropriate legislation.

Amendment 25 (1967)

Section 1 Presidential Succession. In case of the removal of the President from office or his death or resignation, the Vice President shall become President.

Section 2 Vacancies in the Vice Presidency. Whenever there is a vacancy in the office of the Vice President, the President shall nominate a Vice President who shall take the office upon confirmation by a majority vote of both houses of Congress.

Section 3 Disability of the President. Whenever the President transmits to the President pro tempore of the Senate and the Speaker of the House of Representatives his written declaration that he is unable to discharge the powers and duties of his office, and until he transmits to them a written declaration to the contrary, such powers and duties shall be discharged by the Vice President as acting President.

Section 4 Vice President as Acting President. Whenever the Vice President and a majority of either the principal officers of the executive departments, or of such other body as Congress may by law provide, transmit to the president pro tempore of the Senate and the Speaker of the House of Representatives their written declaration that the President is unable to discharge the powers and duties of his office, the Vice President shall immediately assume the powers and duties of the office as acting President.

Thereafter, when the President transmits to the president pro tempore of the Senate and the Speaker of the House of Representatives his written declaration that no inability exists, he shall resume the powers and duties of his office unless the Vice President and a majority of either the principal officers of the executive department, or of such other body as Congress may by law provide, transmit within four days to the president pro tempore of the Senate and the Speaker of the House of Representatives their written declaration that the President is unable to discharge the powers and duties of his office. Thereupon

Congress shall decide the issue, assembling within forty-eight hours for that purpose if not in session. If the Congress, within twenty-one days after receipt of the latter written declaration, or if Congress is not in session, within twenty-one days after Congress is required to assemble, determines by two-thirds vote of both houses that the President is unable to discharge the powers and duties of his office, the Vice President shall continue to discharge the same as acting President; otherwise, the President shall resume the powers and duties of his office.

Amendment 26 (1971)

Section 1 Voting Age. The right of citizens of the United States who are eighteen years of age or older shall not be denied or abridged by the United States or by any state on account of age.

Eighteen-year-olds are given the right to vote.

Section 2 Enforcement. The Congress shall have the power to enforce this article by appropriate legislation.

Congress may pass laws to carry out this amendment.

Amendment 27 (1992)

Congressional Pay Increases. No law varying the compensation for the services of the senators and representatives, shall take effect, until an election of Representatives shall have intervened.

If members of Congress vote themselves a pay raise, that increase cannot go into effect until after the next congressional session.

The Road to Ratification: 1787–1789

1787

FEBRUARY 4
Shays' Rebellion ends.

FEBRUARY 21
Congress of the Confederation endorses a plan to revise Articles of Confederation.

MAY 25
Constitutional Convention opens in Philadelphia.

JUNE 26
The Convention adopts a six-year term for senators.

JULY 12
Roger Sherman proposes the Connecticut Compromise.

AUGUST 6
Committee drafts a constitutional document with 23 articles.

AUGUST 16
Convention grants Congress the right to regulate foreign trade and interstate commerce.

SEPTEMBER 13–15
Convention reviews the draft and makes several changes.

SEPTEMBER 17
Twelve state delegations approve the document.

SEPTEMBER 20
Congress receives the final draft of the Constitution.

SEPTEMBER 28
Congress submits the Constitution to special state conventions for ratification by nine states.

1788

JANUARY 2
Georgia ratifies unanimously.

JANUARY 9
Connecticut ratifies by a vote of 128 to 40.

FEBRUARY 6
The Massachusetts convention ratifies by a vote of 187 to 168.

JUNE 25
Virginia ratifies; Convention endorses a 20-article Bill of Rights plus other changes.

JULY 2
Cyrus Griffin, President of Congress, announces the ratification of the Constitution; preparations begin for the transition to a new government.

JULY 26
New York ratifies by vote of 30 to 27.

AUGUST 2
North Carolina declines to ratify until a Bill of Rights is added.

1789

JANUARY 7
Presidential electors are chosen by ten of the ratifying states.

FEBRUARY 4
Electors choose George Washington as President and John Adams as Vice President.

MARCH 4
First Congress convenes in New York.

AUGUST 7
Congress establishes the War Department.

SEPTEMBER 2
Congress establishes the Treasury Department.

SEPTEMBER 22
Congress creates the office of Postmaster General.

SEPTEMBER 24
Congress passes the Federal Judiciary Act, creating the office of the Attorney General.

MAY 29
Edmund Randolph proposes the Virginia Plan.

JUNE 15
William Paterson proposes the New Jersey Plan.

JUNE 19
Convention decides to discard the Articles, write a new constitution, and create a new national government.

JUNE 21
The Convention adopts a two-year term for representatives.

AUGUST 25
Convention prohibits Congress from banning foreign slave trade for 20 years.

SEPTEMBER 6
Convention adopts a four-year term for the President.

SEPTEMBER 8
Convention appoints a committee to prepare a draft of the complete document.

SEPTEMBER 12
Committee submits the draft to the Convention.

OCTOBER 27
First Federalist Paper, supporting the Constitution, appears in newspapers in New York City.

DECEMBER 7
Delaware ratifies the Constitution, the first state to do so, by unanimous vote.

DECEMBER 12
Pennsylvania ratifies the Constitution, despite opposition.

DECEMBER 18
New Jersey ratifies unanimously.

MARCH 16
Rhode Island holds a popular referendum in which voters reject the Constitution by a vote of 2,708 to 237.

APRIL 28
Maryland ratifies by a vote of 63 to 11.

MAY 23
South Carolina ratifies by a vote of 149 to 73.

JUNE 21
New Hampshire becomes the ninth state to ratify; Convention proposes 12 amendments.

SEPTEMBER 13
New York is selected as the site for the new government; date is set for the first meeting of Congress under the new Constitution.

SEPTEMBER 30
Pennsylvania is the first state to choose its two senators, Robert Morris and William Maclay.

OCTOBER 10
Congress of the Confederation transacts its last official business.

APRIL 1
House of Representatives, with 30 of its members present, elects Frederick Muhlenberg as speaker.

APRIL 6
Senate, with 9 in attendance, chooses John Langdon as temporary presiding officer.

APRIL 30
Washington is inaugurated in New York City as nation's first President.

JULY 27
Congress establishes the Department of Foreign Affairs.

SEPTEMBER 25
Congress submits 12 amendments to the Constitution for ratification by the states.

NOVEMBER 20
New Jersey ratifies 10 of the 12 amendments, the Bill of Rights, the first state to do so.

NOVEMBER 21
North Carolina ratifies the Constitution by vote of 194 to 77.

Name _____ Date _____

1. **Answer the following questions about the Preamble and Article I of the Constitution.**

   a. What is the purpose of the Preamble to the Constitution? _____
   _____

   b. Which branch of the government is described in Article I? _____

   c. What are the requirements for election to the House of Representatives? _____
   _____

   d. What is the length of a representative's term of office? _____

   e. What are the qualifications for election to the Senate? _____
   _____

   f. What is the length of a senator's term of office? _____

   g. How often must Congress meet? _____

2. **Answer the following questions about Article II of the Constitution.**

   a. What are the qualifications for election to the presidency? _____
   _____

   b. What is the length of a President's term of office? _____

   c. What is the President's relationship with the armed forces? _____

   d. Which house of Congress approves many of the President's appointments? _____

3. **Answer the following questions about Article III of the Constitution.**

   a. What is the name of the nation's highest court? _____

   b. How long may Supreme Court justices remain in office? _____

   c. How many witnesses must give testimony to the same act before a person can be convicted of treason?
   _____

4. **Answer the following questions about Articles IV–VII and Amendments
   1–27 of the Constitution.**

   a. Which article specifies how laws are passed? _____

   b. Which article sets forth the method of amending the Constitution? _____

   c. By what name are the first ten amendments commonly known? _____
   _____

   d. Why do you think Amendments 13 through 15 are sometimes called the Civil War amendments?
   _____
   _____

Glossary

A

abolish to end the practice or effect of

abridge to deprive, condense, or reduce in scope

absolute monarch ruler who has complete authority over his or her people

affirmative action policy aimed at ending the effects of past discrimination by giving favored treatment to certain groups, such as minorities and women

amend to change or modify for the better; to improve

B

bail money given to the court by a defendant as security that he or she will return for trial

bankruptcy inability to pay one's debts

bicameral consisting of two legislative chambers

bill of attainder legislative act that inflicts punishment on a person or group without a trial

boycott to avoid using, buying, or dealing with as a means of protest

C

Cabinet presidential advisory board consisting of the heads of the executive departments

capital crime offense that is punishable by death

capital punishment death penalty

censure to officially condemn or express disapproval

charter grant or guarantee of certain rights and privileges to a person, group, or company

checks and balances each branch of government is subject to restraints, or checks, by the other two

citizenship status of a citizen; the rights, privileges, and duties of a member of a community

city-state independent state consisting of a city and its surrounding territory

civil relating to ordinary community life as opposed to criminal proceedings

civil rights constitutional rights guaranteed to all citizens

clause distinct article in a formal document

codify to arrange according to a system; to set down in writing

commission authorization to perform certain official duties

common law legal system based on accepted customs, traditions, and past decisions

compromise settlement of differences in which each side gives up some of its demands in order to reach an agreement

conciliator one who settles disputes or restores friendship between disagreeing parties

constitutionalism basic principle that government and those who govern are bound by law

Continental Congress elected representatives who advised the colonists on policies regarding relations with Britain

convention meeting of delegates for the purpose of conducting business

D

delegate person authorized to act as a representative for others

demigod person of such outstanding qualities as to be almost godlike

democracy system of government in which authority rests with the people

direct democracy system of government in which people participate directly in decision making

discrimination policy or attitude that denies equal rights and treatment to certain groups of people

dissent to disagree or withhold approval

due process principle by which government must act in accordance with established rules

E

elastic clause constitutional power giving Congress the authority to make laws needed to carry out its other responsibilities

eligibility fitness for being chosen; qualification

endow to provide something freely and naturally

Enlightenment period in European history, during the 1700s, characterized by a rejection of traditional, religious, and political ideas in favor of education and reasoning

envoy person delegated to represent a government in its dealings with another nation

establishment clause section of the First Amendment to the Constitution prohibiting the government from setting up a national religion

executive having the power to carry out laws

ex post facto refers to a law applied to events that occurred before the law was passed

extradition process by which a fugitive from justice is returned to the place where the crime occurred

F

federalism division of power between the states and the national government

free exercise clause section of the First Amendment to the Constitution prohibiting the government from interfering in Americans' free exercise of their religious beliefs

G

grand jury group of people selected to hear evidence and decide whether a person should be charged with a crime

grievance cause for complaint

H

habeas corpus right to have charges filed or a hearing before being jailed

high crime serious offense

I

impeach to accuse or formally charge a public official with misconduct

impeachment formal charge brought against a public official

involuntary servitude labor done against one's will

J

Jim Crow laws legislation aimed at isolating and separating a group of people from another based on race

joint resolution legislative measure that must be passed by both houses and approved by the chief executive to become effective; often used for temporary or unusual purposes, such as a constitutional amendment

judicial having the power to interpret and apply the laws

judicial activism practice of basing decisions on what the Court perceives to ensure public welfare, or what the Court determines to be fair and just based on the facts it has been given

judicial restraint practice of basing decisions on previous decisions dealing with similar legal issues, and upholding a law if it does not clearly violate the Constitution

judicial review power of the courts to review the actions of Congress and the President to determine whether they are in accordance with the Constitution

jurisdiction power of a court to try and decide a case; area of authority

L

landmark event or development that marks a turning point

legislative having the power to make laws

legislature lawmaking assembly

letters of marque and reprisal commissions or written grants of power that authorize private citizens to outfit vessels for the capture and destruction of the enemy during wartime

levy to order the payment of

libel publication of statements that wrongfully damage an individual's reputation

limited government idea that government is limited in what it may do and that each citizen has certain rights that cannot be taken away; also called constitutionalism and rule of law

M

militia military force that is on call for service in emergencies

misdemeanor minor offense, such as littering or driving without a license

N

naturalization legal process by which a person born in one country becomes a citizen of another country

nomination process of naming, or selecting, candidates to run for public office

nonsectarian not connected to a particular religious group

O

oath solemn promise

override to prevail over

P

Parliament British law-making body

patrician member of the upper class who traced his ancestry to a senatorial family in the earliest days of the Roman Republic

petition to make a formal request

philosopher person who seeks wisdom and enlightenment; thinker

plea bargain process in which an accused person agrees to plead guilty in exchange for a less serious charge or a lighter sentence

plebeian member of the general body of Roman citizens, as distinct from the upper class

political party organized group that seeks to control government through the winning of elections and the holding of public office

polygamy marriage to more than one person at the same time

popular sovereignty self-government based on the will of the people

preamble introductory statement

precedent legal decision that influences the ruling of later and similar cases

presumption of innocence assumption that an individual is innocent until proven guilty of a crime

probable cause valid reason for police to search or arrest

prosecutor government official who seeks to prove the guilt of an accused person

Q

quorum minimum number of members who must be present for a legislative body to conduct business

quota number or amount making up a proportional share; numerical limit

R

ratify to give formal approval

redress means of seeking a remedy; relief from distress

repeal to revoke or remove by legislative act

representation state of being represented, especially in a legislative body

republic system of government in which people elect representatives to govern them; also known as representative government

republican favoring a republic, or a representative government

resolution formal expression of the opinion of a legislative body

revenue source of income

reverse discrimination unfair treatment of a group of people as a result of an attempt to help another group suffering from previous discriminatory practices

revolutionary favoring great change

rule of law principle that government and those who govern are bound by the fundamental law; constitutionalism

S

salutary neglect policy by which the English monarch allowed the American colonists to rule themselves as long as doing so also benefited England

secular nonreligious; connected with everyday life

segregate to separate people on the basis of race, class, or ethnic background

separation of powers duties and responsibilities of government are divided into three separate but co-equal branches: executive, legislative, and judicial

succession transference of authority on the death of the chief executive

successor person who replaces or follows another

T

tariff charge or tax placed by the government on certain imported goods

tyranny government in which a single ruler has complete control over the people

U

unalienable right freedom that cannot be taken away or transferred to another

unconstitutional not consistent with the Constitution

V

veto to reject or prevent a legislative bill from becoming law

W

writ of habeas corpus court order requiring the government to release a prisoner unless good cause for imprisonment can be shown

writ of mandamus document that mandates, or requires, a public official to perform certain duties

Index

CURRICULUM